# Workshop on Extra-Propositional Aspects of Meaning in Computational Linguistics (ExProM 2016)



Osaka, Japan
12 December 2016

ISBN: 978-1-5108-3330-2

**Printed from e-media with permission by:**

Curran Associates, Inc.
57 Morehouse Lane
Red Hook, NY 12571

**Some format issues inherent in the e-media version may also appear in this print version.**



Printed by Curran Associates, Inc. (2016)

For permission requests, please contact the Association for Computational Linguistics at the address below.

Association for Computational Linguistics
209 N. Eighth Street
Stroudsburg, Pennsylvania 18360

Phone: 1-570-476-8006
Fax: 1-570-476-0860

acl@aclweb.org

**Additional copies of this publication are available from:**

Curran Associates, Inc.
57 Morehouse Lane
Red Hook, NY 12571 USA
Phone: 845-758-0400
Fax: 845-758-2633
Email: curran@proceedings.com
Web: www.proceedings.com

# Preface

During the last decade, semantic representation of text has focused on extracting propositional meaning, i.e., capturing who does what to whom, how, when and where. Several corpora are available, and existing tools extract this kind of knowledge, e.g., semantic role labelers trained on PropBank, NomBank or FrameNet. But propositional semantic representations disregard significant meaning encoded in human language. For example, while sentences (1-2) below share the same propositional meaning regarding verb *carry*, they do not convey the same overall meaning. In order to truly capture what these sentences mean, extra-propositional aspects of meaning (ExProM) such as uncertainty, negation and attribution must be taken into account.

1. Thomas Eric Duncan likely contracted the disease when he carried a pregnant woman sick with Ebola.
2. Thomas Eric personally told me that he never carried a pregnant woman with Ebola.

The Extra-Propositional Aspects of Meaning (ExProM) in Computational Linguistics Workshop focuses on a broad range of semantic phenomena beyond propositional meaning, i.e., beyond linking propositions and their semantic arguments with relations such as AGENT (who), THEME (what), LOCATION (where) and TIME (when).

ExProM is pervasive in human language and, while studied from a theoretical perspective, computational models are scarce. Humans use language to describe events that do not correlate with a real situation in the world. They express desires, intentions and plans, and also discuss events that did not happen or are unlikely to happen. Events are often described hypothetically, and speculation can be used to explain why something is a certain way without a strong commitment. Humans do not always (want to) tell the (whole) truth: they may use deception to hide lies. Devices such as irony and sarcasm are employed to play with words so that what is said is not what is meant. Finally, humans not only describe their personal views or experiences, but also attribute statements to others. These phenomena are not exclusive of opinionated texts. They are ubiquitous in language, including scientific works and news as exemplified below:

- A better team might have prevented this infection.
- Some speculate that this was a failure of the internal communications systems.
- Infected people typically don't become contagious until they develop symptoms.
- Medical personnel can be infected if they don't use protective gear, such as surgical masks and gloves.
- You cannot get it from another person until they start showing symptoms of the disease, like fever.
- You can only catch Ebola from coming into direct contact with the bodily fluids of someone who has the disease and is showing symptoms.
- We've never seen a human virus change the way it is transmitted.
- There is no reason to believe that Ebola virus is any different from any of the viruses that infect humans and have not changed the way that they are spread.

In its 2016 edition, the Extra-Propositional Aspects of Meaning (ExProM) in Computational Linguistics Workshop was collocated with the 26th International Conference on Computational Linguistics (COLING 2016) in Osaka, Japan. The workshop took place on December 12, 2016, and the program consisted of six papers and an invited talk by Preslav Nakov (Qatar Computing Research Institute, HBKU).

ExProM 2016 is a a follow-up of three previous events: the 2010 Negation and Speculation in Natural Language Processing Workshop (NeSp-NLP 2010), ExProM 2012 and ExProM 2015. We would like to thank the authors of papers for their interesting contributions, the members of the program committee for their insightful reviews, and Preslav Nakov for being the invited speaker. We are also grateful to the National Science Foundation for a grant to support student travel to the workshop.

Eduardo Blanco, Roser Morante, and Roser Saurí.

**Organisers**

Eduardo Blanco, University of North Texas, USA
Roser Morante, VU University Amsterdam, The Netherlands
Roser Saurí, Oxford University Press, UK

**Programme Committee**

Mithun Balakrishna - Lymba Corporation
Emily M. Bender - University of Washington
Cosmin Adrian Bejan - Vanderbilt University
Tommaso Caselli - VU University Amsterdam
Marie-Catherine de Marneffe - The Ohio State University
Iris Hendrickx - Radboud University
Lori Levin - Carnegie Mellon University
Erwin Marsi - Norwegian University of Science and Technology
Malvina Nissim - University of Groningen
Christopher Potts - Stanford University
Sampo Pyysalo - University of Cambridge
German Rigau - UPV/EHU
Ellen Riloff - University of Utah
Paolo Rosso - Universitat Politècnica de Valencia
Erik Velldal - University of Oslo
Bonnie Webber - University of Edinburgh

**Invited Speaker**

Preslav Nakov - Qatar Computing Research Institute, HBKU

# Table of Contents

# Workshop Program

**Monday December 12, 2016**

**9:00–9:10** ***Opening remarks***

9:10–9:45 *'Who would have thought of that!': A Hierarchical Topic Model for Extraction of Sarcasm-prevalent Topics and Sarcasm Detection*
Aditya Joshi, Prayas Jain, Pushpak Bhattacharyya and Mark Carman

09:45–10:20 *Detecting Uncertainty Cues in Hungarian Social Media Texts*
Veronika Vincze

**10:20–10:40 Coffee break**

10:40–11:15 *Detecting Level of Belief in Chinese and Spanish*
Juan Pablo Colomer, Keyu Lai and Owen Rambow

11:15–11:50 *Contradiction Detection for Rumorous Claims*
Piroska Lendvai and Uwe Reichel

**11:50–14:00 Lunch break**

***Invited talk***
14:00-15:00 *Negation and Modality in Machine Translation*
Preslav Nakov

**15:00–15:20** ***Coffee break***

15:20–15:55 *Problematic Cases in the Annotation of Negation in Spanish*
Salud María Jiménez-Zafra, Maite Martín, L. Alfonso Ureña Lopez, Toni Martí and Mariona Taulé

15:55–16:30 *Building a Dictionary of Affixal Negations*
Chantal van Son, Emiel van Miltenburg and Roser Morante

**16:30–16:50** ***Discussion and closing remarks***

# 'Who would have thought of that!': A Hierarchical Topic Model for Extraction of Sarcasm-prevalent Topics and Sarcasm Detection

**Aditya Joshi**[1,2,3] **Prayas Jain**[4]
**Pushpak Bhattacharyya**[1] **Mark James Carman**[2]
[1]Indian Institute of Technology Bombay, India, [2]Monash University, Australia
[3]IITB-Monash Research Academy, India, [4]IIT-BHU (Varanasi), India,
{adityaj, pb}@cse.iitb.ac.in ,prayas.jain.cse14@iitbhu.ac.in
mark.carman@monash.edu

## Abstract

Topic Models have been reported to be beneficial for aspect-based sentiment analysis. This paper reports a simple topic model for sarcasm detection, a first, to the best of our knowledge. Designed on the basis of the intuition that sarcastic tweets are likely to have a mixture of words of both sentiments as against tweets with literal sentiment (either positive or negative), our hierarchical topic model discovers sarcasm-prevalent topics and topic-level sentiment. Using a dataset of tweets labeled using hashtags, the model estimates topic-level, and sentiment-level distributions. Our evaluation shows that topics such as 'work', 'gun laws', 'weather' are sarcasm-prevalent topics. Our model is also able to discover the mixture of sentiment-bearing words that exist in a text of a given sentiment-related label. Finally, we apply our model to predict sarcasm in tweets. We outperform two prior work based on statistical classifiers with specific features, by around 25%.

## 1 Introduction

Sarcasm detection is the computational task of predicting sarcasm in text. Past approaches in sarcasm detection rely on designing classifiers with specific features (to capture sentiment changes or incorporate context about the author, environment, etc.) (Joshi et al., 2015; Wallace et al., 2014; Rajadesingan et al., 2015; Bamman and Smith, 2015), or model conversations using the sequence labeling-based approach by Joshi et al. (2016c). Approaches, in addition to this statistical classifier-based paradigm are: deep learning-based approaches as in the case of Silvio Amir et al. (2016) or rule-based approaches such as Riloff et al. (2013; Khattri et al. (2015).

This work *employs a machine learning technique that, to the best of our knowledge, has not been used for computational sarcasm. Specifically, we introduce a topic model for extraction of sarcasm-prevalent topics and as a result, for sarcasm detection.* Our model based on a supervised version of the Latent Dirichlet Allocation (LDA) model (Blei et al., 2003) is able to discover clusters of words that correspond to sarcastic topics. The goal of this work is to discover sarcasm-prevalent topics based on sentiment distribution within text, and use these topics to improve sarcasm detection. The key idea of the model is that (a) some topics are more likely to be sarcastic than others, and (b) sarcastic tweets are likely to have a different distribution of positive-negative words as compared to literal positive or negative tweets. Hence, distribution of sentiment in a tweet is the central component of our model.

Our sarcasm topic model is learned on tweets that are labeled with three sentiment labels: literal positive, literal negative and sarcastic. In order to extract sarcasm-prevalent topics, the model uses three latent variables: a topic variable to indicate words that are prevalent in sarcastic discussions, a sentiment variable for sentiment-bearing words related to a topic, and a switch variable that switches between the two kinds of words (topic and sentiment-bearing words). Using a dataset of 166,955 tweets, our model is able to discover words corresponding to topics that are found in our corpus of positive, negative and sarcastic tweets.

We evaluate our model in two steps: a **qualitative evaluation** that ascertains sarcasm-prevalent topics based on the ones extracted, and a **quantitative evaluation** that evaluates sub-components of the model. We also demonstrate how it can be used for sarcasm detection. To do so, we compare our model with two prior work, and observe a significant improvement of around 25% in the F-score.



*Proceedings of the Workshop on Extra-Propositional Aspects of Meaning in Computational Linguistics,*
pages 1–10, Osaka, Japan, December 12 2016.

The rest of the paper is organized as follows. Section 2 discusses the related work. Section 3 presents our motivation for using topic models for automatic sarcasm detection. Section 4 describes the design rationale and structure of our model. Section 5 describes the dataset and the experiment setup. Section 6 discusses the results in three steps: qualitative results, quantitative results and application of our topic model to sarcasm detection. Section 7 concludes the paper and points to future work.

## 2 Related Work

Topic models are popular for sentiment aspect extraction. Jo and Oh (2011) present an aspect-sentiment unification model that learns different aspects of a product, and the words that are used to express sentiment towards the aspects. In terms of using two latent variables: one for aspect and one for sentiment, they are related to our model. Mukherjee and Liu (2012a) use a semi-supervised model in order to extract aspect-level sentiment. The role of the supervised sentiment label in our model is similar to their work. Finally, McAuley and Leskovec (2013a) attempt to generate rating dimensions of products using topic models. However, the topic models that have been reported in past work have been for sentiment analysis in general. They do not have any special consideration to either sarcasm as a label or sarcastic tweets as a special case of tweets. The hierarchy-based structure (specifically, the chain of distributions for sentiment label) in our model is based on Joshi et al. (2016a) who extract politically relevant topics from a dataset of political tweets. The chain in their case is sentiment distribution of an individual and a group.

Sarcasm detection approaches have also been reported in the past (Joshi et al., 2016b; Liebrecht et al., 2013; Wang et al., 2015; Joshi et al., 2015). Wang et al. (2015) present a contextual model for sarcasm detection that collectively models a set of tweets, using a sequence labeling algorithm - however, the goal is to detect sarcasm in the last tweet in the sequence. The idea of distribution of sentiment that we use in our model is based on the idea of context incongruity. In order to evaluate the benefit of our model to sarcasm detection, we compare two sarcasm detection approaches based on our model with two prior work, namely by Buschmeier et al. (2014) and Liebrecht et al. (2013). Buschmeier et al. (2014) train their classifiers using features such as unigrams, laughter expressions, hyperbolic expressions, etc. Liebrecht et al. (2013) experiment with unigrams, bigrams and trigrams as features. To the best of our knowledge, past approaches for sarcasm detection do not use topic modeling, which we do.

## 3 Motivation

Topic models enable discovery of thematic structures in a large-sized corpus. The motivation behind using topic models for sarcasm detection arises from two reasons: (a) presence of sarcasm-prevalent topics, and (b) differences in sentiment distribution in sarcastic and non-sarcastic text. In context of sentiment analysis, topic models have been used for aspect-based sentiment analysis in order to discover topic and sentiment words (Jo and Oh, 2011). The general idea is that for a restaurant review, the word 'spicy' is more likely to describe food as against ambiance. On similar lines, the discovery that a set of words belong to a sarcasm-prevalent topic - a topic regarding which sarcastic remarks are common - can be useful as additional information to a sarcasm detection system. The key idea of our approach is that some topics are more likely to evoke sarcasm than some others. For example, a tweet about working late night at office/ doing school homework till late night is much more probable to be sarcastic than a tweet on Mother's Day. A sarcasm detection system can benefit from incorporating this information about sarcasm-prevalent topics. The second reason is the difference in sentiment distributions. A positive tweet is likely to contain only positive words, a negative tweet is likely to contain only negative words. On the other hand, a sarcastic tweet may contain a mix of the two kind of words (for example, '*I love being ignored*' where '*love*' is a positive word and '*ignored*' is a negative word), except in the case of hyperbolic sarcasm (for example '*This is the best movie ever!*' where '*best*' is a positive word and there is no negative word). Hence, in addition to sarcasm-prevalent topics, sentiment distributions for tweets also form a critical component of our topic model.

| **Observed Variables and Distributions** | |
|---|---|
| $w$ | Word in a tweet |
| $l$ | Label of a tweet; takes values: positive, negative, sarcastic) |
| **Distributions** | |
| $\eta_w$ | Distribution over switch values given a word w |
| **Latent Variables and Distributions** | |
| $z$ | Topic of a tweet |
| $s$ | Sentiment of a word in a tweet; takes values: positive, negative |
| $is$ | Switch variable indicating whether a word is a topic word or a sentiment word; takes values: 0, 1 |
| **Distributions** | |
| $\theta_l$ | Distribution over topics given a label l, with prior $\alpha$ |
| $\phi_z$ | Distribution over words given a topic z and switch =0 (topic word), with prior $\gamma$ |
| $\chi_s$ | Distribution over words given sentiment s and switch=1 (sentiment word), with prior $\delta_1$ |
| $\chi_{sz}$ | Distribution over words given a sentiment s and topic z and switch=1 (sentiment word), with prior $\delta_2$ |
| $\psi_l$ | Distribution over sentiment given a label l and switch =1 (sentiment word), with prior $\beta_1$ |
| $\psi_{zl}$ | Distribution over sentiment given a label l and topic z and switch =1 (sentiment word), with prior $\beta_2$ |

Table 1: Glossary of Variables/Distributions used

## 4 Sarcasm Topic Model

### 4.1 Design Rationale

Our topic model requires sentiment labels of tweets, as used in Ramage et al. (2009). This sentiment can be positive or negative. However, in order to incorporate sarcasm, we re-organize the two sentiment values into three: literal positive, literal negative and sarcastic. The observed variable $l$ in our model indicates this sentiment label. *For sake of simplicity, we refer to the three values of $l$ as positive, negative and sarcastic, in rest of the paper.*

Every word $w$ in a tweet is either a topic word or a sentiment word. A topic word arises due to a topic, whereas a sentiment word arises due to combination of topic and sentiment. This notion is common to several sentiment-based topic models from past work (Jo and Oh, 2011). To determine which of the two (topic or sentiment word) a given word is, our model uses three latent variables: a tweet-level topic label $z$, a word-level sentiment label $s$, and a switch variable $is$. Each tweet is assumed to have a single topic indicated by $z$. The single-topic assumption is reasonable considering the length of a tweet. At the word level, we introduce two variables $is$ and $s$. For each word in the dictionary, $is$ denotes the probability of the word being a topic word or a sentiment word. Thus, the model estimates three sets of distributions: (A) Probability of a word belonging to topic ($\phi_z$) or sentiment-topic combination ($\chi_{sz}$), (B) Sentiment distributions over label and topic ($\psi_{zl}$), and (C) Topic distributions over label ($\theta_l$). The switch variable $is$ is sampled from $\eta_w$, the probability of the word being a topic word or a sentiment word. We thus allow a word to be either a topic word or a sentiment word.[1]

### 4.2 Plate Diagram

Our sarcasm topic model to extract sarcasm-prevalent topics is based on supervised LDA (Blei et al., 2003). Figure 1 shows the plate diagram while Table 1 details the variables and distributions in the model. Every tweet consists of a set of observed words $w$ and one tweet-level, observed sentiment label $l$. The label takes **three** values: positive, negative or sarcastic. The third label value 'sarcastic' indicates a scenario where a tweet appears positive on the surface but is implicitly negative (hence, sarcastic). $z$ is a tweet-level latent variable, denoting the topic of the tweet. The number of topics, $Z$ is experimentally determined. $is$ is a word-level latent variable representing if a word is a topic word or a sentiment word,

[1]Note that $\eta_w$ is not estimated during the sampling but learned from a large-scale corpus, as will be described later.

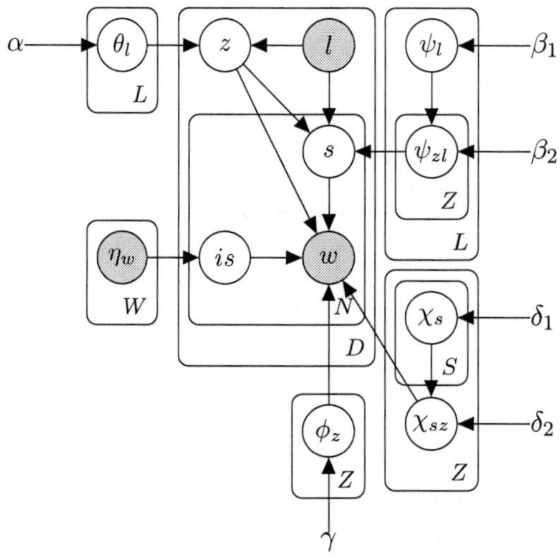


Figure 1: Plate Diagram of Sarcasm Topic Model

similar to Mukherjee and Liu (2012c). If the word is a sentiment word, the word-level latent variable $s$ represents the sentiment of that word. It can take $S$ unique values. Intuitively, $S$ is set as 2.

Among the distributions, $\eta_w$ is an observed distribution that is estimated beforehand. It denotes the probability of the word $w$ being a topic word or a sentiment word. Distribution $\theta_l$ represents the distribution over $z$ given the label of the tweet as $l$. $\psi_l$ and $\psi_{zl}$ are an hierarchical pair of distributions. $\psi_{zl}$ represents the distribution over sentiment of the word given the topic and label of the tweet and that the word is a sentiment word. $\chi_s$ and $\chi_{sz}$ are an hierarchical pair of distributions , where $\chi_{sz}$ represents distribution over words, given the word is a sentiment word with sentiment $s$ and topic $z$. $\phi_z$ is a distribution over words given the word is an topic word with topic $z$. The generative story of our model is:

1. *For each label $l$, select* $\vec{\theta}_l \sim Dir(\alpha)$
2. *For each label $l$, select* $\vec{\psi}_l \sim Dir(\beta_1)$
   *For each topic $z$, select*
   $\vec{\psi}_{l,z} \sim Dir(\beta_2 \vec{\psi}_l)$
3. *For each topic $z$ and sentiment $s$, select* $\vec{\chi}_s \sim Dir(\delta_1)$*, and* $\vec{\chi}_{s,z} \sim Dir(\delta_2 \vec{\chi}_s)$
4. *For each topic $z$ select* $\vec{\phi}_z \sim Dir(\gamma)$
5. *For each tweet $k$ select*
   (a) *topic* $z_k \sim \vec{\theta}_{l_k}$
   (b) *switch value for all words,* $is_{k_j} \sim \vec{\eta}_j$
   (c) *sentiment for all sentiment words,* $s_{kj} \sim \vec{\psi}_{z_k, l_k}$
   (d) *all topic words,* $w_{kj} \sim \vec{\phi}_{z_k}$
   (e) *all sentiment words,* $w_{kj} \sim \vec{\chi}_{s_{kj}, z_k}$

We estimate these distribution using Gibbs sampling. The joint probability over all variables is decomposed into these distributions, based on dependencies in the model. Estimation details have not been included due to lack of space.

## 5 Experiment Setup

We create a dataset of English tweets for our topic model. We do not use datasets reported in past work (related to classifiers) because topic models typically require larger datasets than classifiers. The tweets are downloaded from twitter using the twitter API[2] using hashtag-based supervision. Hashtag-based supervision is common in sarcasm-labeled datasets (Joshi et al., 2015). Tweets containing hashtags #happy, #excited are labeled as positive tweets. Tweets with #sad, #angry are labeled as negative tweets. Tweets with #sarcasm and #sarcastic are labeled as sarcastic tweets. The tweets are converted to lowercase, and the hashtags used for supervision are removed. Function words[3], punctuation, hashtags, author names

[2] https://dev.twitter.com/rest/public

[3] www.sequencepublishing.com

and hyperlinks are removed from the tweets. Duplicate tweets (same tweet text repeated for multiple tweets) and re-tweets (tweet text with the 'RT' added in the beginning) are discarded. Finally, words which occur less than three times in the vocabulary are also removed. As a result, the tweets that have less than 3 words are removed. This results in a dataset of 166,955 tweets. Out of these, 70,934 are positive, 20,253 are negative and the remaining 75,769 are sarcastic. A total of 35398 tweets are used for testing, out of which 26,210 are of positive sentiment, 5535 are of negative sentiment and 3653 are sarcastic. We repeat that these labels are determined based on hashtags, as stated above.

The total number of distinct labels ($L$) is 3, and the total number of distinct sentiment ($S$) is 2. The total number of distinct topics ($Z$) is experimentally determined as 50. We use block-based Gibbs sampling to estimate the distributions. The block-based sampler samples all latent variables together based on their joint distributions. We set asymmetric priors based on sentiment word-list from McAuley and Leskovec (2013b).

A key parameter of the model is $\eta_w$ since it drives the split of a word as a topic or a sentiment word. SentiWordNet (Baccianella et al., 2010) is used to learn the distribution $\eta_w$ prior to estimating the model. We average across multiple senses of a word. Based on the SentiWordNet scores to all senses of a word, we determine this probability.

## 6 Results

| Work | Party | Jokes | Weather |
|---|---|---|---|
| day | life | Quote | Snow |
| morning | friends | Jokes | Today |
| night | night | Humor | Rain |
| today | drunk | Comedy | Weather |
| work | parties | Satire | Day |
| **Women** | **School** | **Love** | **Politics** |
| Women | tomorrow | love | Ukraine |
| Wife | school | feeling | Russia |
| Compliment(s) | work | break-up | again |
| Fashion | morning | day/night | deeply |
| Love | night | sleep | raiders |

Table 2: Topics estimated when the topic model is learned on only sarcastic tweets

### 6.1 Qualitative Evaluation

The goal of this section is to present topics discovered by our sarcasm topic model. We do so in two steps. We first describe the topics generated when only sarcastic tweets from our corpus are used to estimate the distributions, followed by the ones when the full corpus is used. In case of the former, since only sarcastic tweets are used, the topics generated here indicate words corresponding to sarcasm-prevalent topics. In case of the latter, the sentiment-topic distributions in the model capture the prevalence of sarcasm.

The model estimates the $\phi$ and $\chi$ distributions corresponding to topic words and sentiment words. Top five words for a subset of topics (as estimated by $\phi$) are shown in Table 2. The headings in boldface are manually assigned[4]. Sarcasm-prevalent topics, as discovered by our topic model, are work, party, weather, women, etc. The corresponding sentiment topics for each of these sarcasm-prevalent topics (as estimated by $\chi$) are given in Table 3. The headings in boldface are manually assigned. For topics corresponding to 'party' and 'women', we observe that the two columns contain words from opposing sentiment polarities. An example sarcastic tweet about work is 'Yaay! Another night spent at office! I love working late night'.

The previous set of topics are all from sarcastic text. We now show the topics extracted by our model from the full corpus. These topics will indicate peculiarity of topics for each of the three labels, allowing

[4]This is a common practice in topics model papers, in order to interpret topics. (Mukherjee and Liu, 2012b; Joshi et al., 2016a; Kim et al., 2013)

| **Work** | | **Party** | | **Jokes** | | **Weather** | |
|---|---|---|---|---|---|---|---|
| Love | Great | Lol | Hate | Funny | Lol | Love | nice |
| Good | Sick | Attractive | Allergic | Liar | Fucks | Glad | wow |
| Awesome | Seriously | Love | Insulting | Hilarious | Like | Fun | really |
| **Women** | | **School** | | **Love** | | **Politics** | |
| Compliment(s) | Talents | excited | fun | best | love | Losing | issues |
| Thrilled | Sorry | love | omg | awesome | ignored | lies | weep |
| Recognized | Bad | really | awesome | greatest | sick | like | really |

Table 3: Sentiment-related topics estimated when the topic model is learned on only sarcastic tweets

| **Music** | **work/school** | **Orlando Incident** | **Holiday** | **Quotes** | **Food** |
|---|---|---|---|---|---|
| pop | work | orlando | summer | quote(s) | food |
| country | sleep | shooting | wekend | morning | lunch |
| rock | night | prayers | holiday | inspiration | vegan |
| bluegrass | morning | families | friends | motivation | breakfast |
| beatles | school | victims | sun,beach | mind | cake |

| **Stock(s)/ Commodities** | **Father** | **Gun** | **Pets** | **Health** |
|---|---|---|---|---|
| silver | father(s) | gun(s) | dog | fitness |
| gold | dad | orlando | cat | gym |
| index | daddy | trump | baby | run |
| price | family | shooting | puppy | morning |
| consumer | work | muslim | pets | health |

Table 4: Topics estimated when the topic model is learned on full corpus

us to infer what topics are sarcasm-prevalent. Table 4 shows the top 5 topic words for the topics discovered (as estimated in $\phi$) from the full corpus (*i.e.*, containing tweets of all three tweet-level sentiment labels: positive, negative and sarcastic). Table 5 shows the top 3 sentiment words for each sentiment (as estimated by $\chi$) of each of the topics discovered. Like in the previous case, the heading in boldface is manually assigned. One of the topic discovered was 'Music'. The top 5 topic words for the topic 'Music' are Pop, Country, Rock, Bluegrass and Beatles. The corresponding sentiment words for Music are 'love', 'happy', 'good' on the positive side and 'sad', 'passion' and 'pain' on the negative side.

The **remaining sections present results when the model is learned on the full corpus**.

### 6.2 Quantitative Evaluation

In this section, we answer three questions: (A) What is the likely sentiment label, if a user is talking about a particular topic? (Section 6.2.1), (B) We hypothesize that sarcastic text tends to have mixed-polarity

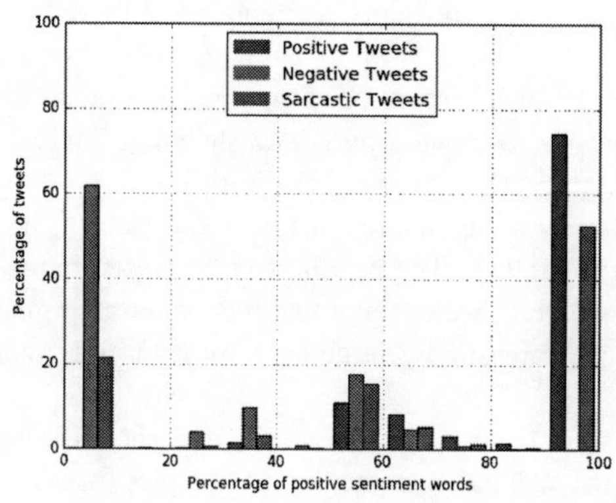


Figure 2: Distribution of word-level sentiment labels for tweet-level labels

| Stock(s)/ Commodities | | Father | | Gun | | Pets | | Health | | Music | |
|---|---|---|---|---|---|---|---|---|---|---|---|
| gains | risks | happy | lol | like | sad | happy | small | love | tired | love | sad |
| happiness | dipped | love | little | good | hate | love | sad | fun | sick | happy | passion |
| unchanged | down | best | bless | wow | angry | cute | miss | laugh | unfit | good | pain |

| Work/School | | Orlando Incident | | Holiday | | Quotes | | Food | |
|---|---|---|---|---|---|---|---|---|---|
| great | sick | love | tragedy | love | beauty | positive | simple | happy | foodie |
| fun | hate | like | hate | smile | hot | happy | kind | yummy | seriously |
| yay | ugh | want | heartbroken | fun | sexy | happiness | sad | healthy | perfect |

Table 5: Sentiment-related topics estimated when the topic model is learned on full corpus

| Topics P(l/z) | Positive | Negative | Sarcastic |
|---|---|---|---|
| Holiday | **0.9538** | 0.0140 | 0.0317 |
| Father | **0.9224** | 0.0188 | 0.0584 |
| Quote | **0.8782** | 0.0363 | 0.0852 |
| Food | **0.8100** | 0.0331 | 0.1566 |
| Music | **0.7895** | 0.0743 | 0.1363 |
| Fitness | **0.7622** | 0.0431 | 0.1948 |
| Orlando Incident | 0.0130 | **0.9500** | 0.0379 |
| Gun | 0.1688 | 0.3074 | **0.5230** |
| Work | 0.1089 | 0.0354 | **0.8554** |
| Humor | 0.0753 | 0.1397 | **0.7841** |

Table 6: Probability of sentiment label for various discovered topics

words. Does it hold in case of our model? (Section 6.2.2), and (C) How can sarcasm topic model be used for sarcasm detection? (Section 6.2.3).

### 6.2.1 Probability of sentiment label, given topic

We compute the probability $p(l/z)$ based on the model. Table 6 shows these values for a subset of topics. Topics with a majority positive sentiment are Father's Day (0.9224), holidays (0.9538), etc. The topic with the highest probability of a negative sentiment is the Orlando shooting incident (0.95). Gun laws (0.5230), work and humor are where sarcasm is prevalent.

### 6.2.2 Distribution of sentiment words for tweet-level sentiment labels

Figure 2 shows the proportion of word-level sentiment labels, for the three tweet-level sentiment labels, **as estimated by our model**. The X-axis indicates percentage of positive sentiment words in a tweet, while Y-axis indicates percentage of tweets which indicate a specific value of percentage. More than 60% negative tweets (bar in red) have 0% positive content words. The 'positive' here indicates the value of $s$ for a word in a tweet. In other words, the said red bar indicates that 60% tweets have 0% words sampled with $s$ as positive.

It follows intuition that negative tweets have low percentage of positive words (red bar on the left part of the graph) while positive tweets have high percentage of positive words (blue bar on the right part of the graph). The interesting variations are observed in case of sarcastic tweets. It must be highlighted that *the sentiment labels considered for these proportions are* ***as estimated by our topic model***. Many sarcastic tweets contain very high percentage of positive sentiment words. Similarly, the proportion of tweets with around 50% positive sentiment words is around 20%, as expected. Thus, the model is able to capture the sentiment mixture as expected in the three tweet-level sentiment labels: (literal) positive, (literal) negative and sarcastic.

### 6.2.3 Application to Sarcasm Detection

We now use our sarcasm topic model to detect sarcasm, and compare it with two prior work. The task here is to classify a tweets as either sarcastic or not. We use the topic model for sarcasm detection using two methods:

1. **Log-likelihood based**: The topic model is first learned using the training corpus where the distributions in the model are estimated. Then, the topic model performs sampling for a pre-determined number of samples, in three runs - once for each label. For each run, the log-likelihood of the tweet given the estimated distributions (in the training phase) and the sampled values of the latent variables (for this tweet) is computed. The label of the tweet is returned as the one with the highest log-likelihood.

2. **Sampling-based**: Like in the previous case, the topic model first estimates distributions using the training corpus. Then, the topic model is learned again where the label $l$ is assumed to be latent, in addition to the tweet-level latent variable $z$, and word-level latent variables $s$, and $is$. The value of $l$ as learned by the sampler is returned as the predicted label.

We compare our results with two previously existing techniques, Buschmeier et al. (2014) and Liebrecht et al. (2013). We ensure that our implementations result in performance comparable to the reported papers. The two rely on designing sarcasm-level features, and training classifiers for these features. For these classifiers, the positive and negative labels are combined as non-sarcastic. As stated above, the test set is separate from the training set. The results of these two past methods compared with the two based on topic models are shown in Table 7. The values are averaged over the two classes. Both prior work show poor F-score (around 18-19%) while our sampling based approach achieves the best F-score of 46.80%. The low values, in general, may be because our corpus is large in size, and is diverse in terms of the topics. Also, features in Liebrecht et al. (2013) are unigrams, bigrams and trigrams which may result in sparse features.

| **Approach** | **P (%)** | **R (%)** | **F (%)** |
|---|---|---|---|
| (Buschmeier et al., 2014) | 10.41 | 100.00 | 18.85 |
| (Liebrecht et al., 2013) | 11.03 | 99.88 | 19.86 |
| Topic Model: Log Likelihood | 46.40 | 46.56 | 46.48 |
| Topic Model: Sampling | 45.94 | 47.70 | **46.80** |

Table 7: Comparison of Various Approaches for Sarcasm Detection

## 7 Conclusion & Future Work

We presented a novel topic model that discovers sarcasm-prevalent topics. Our topic model uses a dataset of tweets (labeled as positive, negative and sarcastic), and estimates distributions corresponding to prevalence of a topic, prevalence of a sentiment-bearing words. We observed that topics such as work, weather, politics, etc. were discovered as sarcasm-prevalent topics. We evaluated the model in three steps: (a) Based on the distributions learned by our model, we show the most likely label, for all topics. This is to understand sarcasm-prevalence of topics when the model is learned on the full corpus. (b) We then show distribution of word-level sentiment for each tweet-level sentiment label as estimated by our model. *Our intuition that sentiment distribution in a tweet is different for the three labels: positive, negative and sarcastic, holds true.* (c) Finally, we show how topics from this topic model can be harnessed for sarcasm detection. We implement two approaches: one based on most likely label as per log likelihood, and another based on last sampled value during iteration. In both the cases, we are able to significantly outperform two prior work based on feature design by F-Score of around 25%.

The current model is limited because of its key intuition about sentiment mixture in sarcastic text. Instances such as hyperbolic sarcasm go against the intuition. The current approach relies only on bag of words which may be extended to n-grams since a lot of sarcasm is expressed through phrases with implied sentiment. This work, being an initial work in topic models for sarcasm, sets up the promise of topic models for sarcasm detection, as also demonstrated in corresponding work in aspect-based sentiment analysis.

## References


Stefano Baccianella, Andrea Esuli, and Fabrizio Sebastiani. 2010. Sentiwordnet 3.0: An enhanced lexical resource for sentiment analysis and opinion mining. In *LREC*, volume 10, pages 2200–2204.

David Bamman and Noah A Smith. 2015. Contextualized sarcasm detection on twitter. In *Ninth International AAAI Conference on Web and Social Media*.

David M Blei, Andrew Y Ng, and Michael I Jordan. 2003. Latent dirichlet allocation. *Journal of machine Learning research*, 3(Jan):993–1022.

Konstantin Buschmeier, Philipp Cimiano, and Roman Klinger. 2014. An impact analysis of features in a classification approach to irony detection in product reviews. In *Proceedings of the 5th Workshop on Computational Approaches to Subjectivity, Sentiment and Social Media Analysis*, pages 42–49.

Yohan Jo and Alice H Oh. 2011. Aspect and sentiment unification model for online review analysis. In *Proceedings of the fourth ACM international conference on Web search and data mining*, pages 815–824. ACM.

Aditya Joshi, Vinita Sharma, and Pushpak Bhattacharyya. 2015. Harnessing context incongruity for sarcasm detection. In *Proceedings of the 53rd Annual Meeting of the Association for Computational Linguistics and the 7th International Joint Conference on Natural Language Processing*, volume 2, pages 757–762.

Aditya Joshi, Pushpak Bhattacharyya, and Mark Carman. 2016a. Political issue extraction model: A novel hierarchical topic model that uses tweets by political and non-political authors. In *7th Workshop on Computational Approaches to Subjectivity, Sentiment & Social Media Analysis*, pages 82–90.

Aditya Joshi, Pushpak Bhattacharyya, and Mark James Carman. 2016b. Automatic sarcasm detection: A survey. *arXiv preprint arXiv:1602.03426*.

Aditya Joshi, Vaibhav Tripathi, Pushpak Bhattacharyya, and Mark Carman. 2016c. Harnessing sequence labeling for sarcasm detection in dialogue from tv series 'friends'. *CoNLL 2016*, page 146.

Anupam Khattri, Aditya Joshi, Pushpak Bhattacharyya, and Mark James Carman. 2015. Your sentiment precedes you: Using an author's historical tweets to predict sarcasm. In *6TH WORKSHOP ON COMPUTATIONAL APPROACHES TO SUBJECTIVITY, SENTIMENT AND SOCIAL MEDIA ANALYSIS WASSA 2015*, page 25.

Suin Kim, Jianwen Zhang, Zheng Chen, Alice H Oh, and Shixia Liu. 2013. A hierarchical aspect-sentiment model for online reviews. In *AAAI*.

CC Liebrecht, FA Kunneman, and APJ van den Bosch. 2013. The perfect solution for detecting sarcasm in tweets# not.

Julian McAuley and Jure Leskovec. 2013a. Hidden factors and hidden topics: understanding rating dimensions with review text. In *Proceedings of the 7th ACM conference on Recommender systems*, pages 165–172. ACM.

Julian John McAuley and Jure Leskovec. 2013b. From amateurs to connoisseurs: modeling the evolution of user expertise through online reviews. In *Proceedings of the 22nd international conference on World Wide Web*, pages 897–908. International World Wide Web Conferences Steering Committee.

Arjun Mukherjee and Bing Liu. 2012a. Aspect extraction through semi-supervised modeling. In *Proceedings of the 50th Annual Meeting of the Association for Computational Linguistics: Long Papers-Volume 1*, pages 339–348. Association for Computational Linguistics.

Arjun Mukherjee and Bing Liu. 2012b. Aspect extraction through semi-supervised modeling. In *Proceedings of the 50th Annual Meeting of the Association for Computational Linguistics: Long Papers-Volume 1*, pages 339–348. Association for Computational Linguistics.

Arjun Mukherjee and Bing Liu. 2012c. Modeling review comments. In *Proceedings of the 50th Annual Meeting of the Association for Computational Linguistics: Long Papers-Volume 1*, pages 320–329. Association for Computational Linguistics.

Ashwin Rajadesingan, Reza Zafarani, and Huan Liu. 2015. Sarcasm detection on twitter: A behavioral modeling approach. In *Proceedings of the Eighth ACM International Conference on Web Search and Data Mining*, WSDM '15, pages 97–106, New York, NY, USA. ACM.

Daniel Ramage, David Hall, Ramesh Nallapati, and Christopher D. Manning. 2009. Labeled lda: A supervised topic model for credit attribution in multi-labeled corpora. In *Proceedings of the 2009 Conference on Empirical Methods in Natural Language Processing: Volume 1 - Volume 1*, EMNLP '09, pages 248–256, Stroudsburg, PA, USA. Association for Computational Linguistics.

Ellen Riloff, Ashequl Qadir, Prafulla Surve, Lalindra De Silva, Nathan Gilbert, and Ruihong Huang. 2013. Sarcasm as contrast between a positive sentiment and negative situation. In *EMNLP*, volume 13, pages 704–714.

Byron C Silvio Amir, Wallace, Hao Lyu, and Paula Carvalho Mário J Silva. 2016. Modelling context with user embeddings for sarcasm detection in social media. *CoNLL 2016*, page 167.

Byron C. Wallace, Do Kook Choe, Laura Kertz, and Eugene Charniak. 2014. Humans require context to infer ironic intent (so computers probably do, too). In *Proceedings of the 52nd Annual Meeting of the Association for Computational Linguistics (Volume 2: Short Papers)*, pages 512–516, Baltimore, Maryland, June. Association for Computational Linguistics.

Zelin Wang, Zhijian Wu, Ruimin Wang, and Yafeng Ren. 2015. Twitter sarcasm detection exploiting a context-based model. In *Web Information Systems Engineering–WISE 2015*, pages 77–91. Springer.

# Detecting Uncertainty Cues in Hungarian Social Media Texts

**Veronika Vincze**[1,2]
[1]Institute of Informatics, University of Szeged
Árpád tér 2., 6720 Szeged, Hungary
[2]MTA-SZTE Research Group on Artificial Intelligence
Tisza Lajos krt. 103., 6720 Szeged, Hungary
vinczev@inf.u-szeged.hu

## Abstract

In this paper, we aim at identifying uncertainty cues in Hungarian social media texts. We present our machine learning based uncertainty detector which is based on a rich features set including lexical, morphological, syntactic, semantic and discourse-based features, and we evaluate our system on a small set of manually annotated social media texts. We also carry out cross-domain and domain adaptation experiments using an annotated corpus of standard Hungarian texts and show that domain differences significantly affect machine learning. Furthermore, we argue that differences among uncertainty cue types may also affect the efficiency of uncertainty detection.

## 1 Introduction

In several fields of natural language processing, the factuality of information plays an important role (Morante and Sporleder, 2012). Factual and non-factual information should be treated separately, more precisely, negated or speculative/uncertain information should not be mixed up with factual information. For instance, search engines should not retrieve documents where the information in question is negated or unreliable. Uncertainty detectors can help select reliable (certain) and unreliable (uncertain) parts of documents. Thus, developing uncertainty detectors is highly desirable for many fields of NLP (Morante and Sporleder, 2012; Farkas et al., 2010).

With the advent of Web2.0, many social media platforms have become widely popular, which means that a huge amount of user generated textual content appears on the web on a daily basis in the form of weblog posts, Facebook posts and comments, tweets etc. The majority of these contributions is published freely, i.e. without moderation, and even if they are moderated, moderators usually seek for utterances that violate the norms of the given page by using bad language or words that might hurt others' feelings. However, the reliability of the content of user generated data has hardly been investigated, in other words, social media users can publish whatever they want to and the factuality and (un)certainty of these contents may be an issue for those in need of collecting information from the web.

In this paper, we aim at identifying uncertainty cues in social media texts. We focus on Hungarian, a morphologically rich language. Later, we present our machine learning based uncertainty detector. We evaluate our system on a small set of manually annotated social media texts and we compare our results with those obtained by earlier experiments on Hungarian (Vincze, 2014). Finally, we also carry out some cross domain and domain adaptation experiments and we argue that data sparsity may be overcome by simple domain adaptation techniques.

The main contributions of this paper are the following:

- we report the first results on uncertainty detection in Hungarian social media texts;
- we introduce new features in the machine learning setting developed for the linguistic characteristics of social media texts;





*Proceedings of the Workshop on Extra-Propositional Aspects of Meaning in Computational Linguistics*, pages 11–21, Osaka, Japan, December 12 2016.

- we carry out cross domain and domain adaptation experiments and show that domain differences significantly affect machine learning;
- we argue that linguistic features of uncertainty cue types may also affect the efficiency of uncertainty detection;
- we argue that the efficiency of machine learning can be improved by adding out-domain data to the training.

## 2 Related Work

Uncertainty detection has recently gained popularity in the NLP literature. The CoNLL-2010 Shared Task aimed at detecting uncertainty cues in biological papers and Wikipedia articles written in English (Farkas et al., 2010). More recently, a special issue of the journal Computational Linguistics (Vol. 38, No. 2) was dedicated to detecting modality and negation in natural language texts (Morante and Sporleder, 2012).

Among the systems for uncertainty detection we can find rule-based ones (Light et al., 2004; Chapman et al., 2007) but also those based on machine learning methods, usually applying a supervised approach. Some of them used token classification (Morante and Daelemans, 2009; Sánchez et al., 2010; Fernandes et al., 2010; Clausen, 2010) or sequence labeling approaches (Zhang et al., 2010; Li et al., 2010; Rei and Briscoe, 2010; Tang et al., 2010). Özgür and Radev (2009) and Velldal (2010) matched cues from a lexicon then applied a binary classifier based on features describing the context of the cue candidate. Most of these systems focus on the English language, however, we are aware of a study aiming at detecting uncertainty in Hungarian texts (Vincze, 2014).

Supervised machine learning methods were carried out on corpora from different domains such as biology (Medlock and Briscoe, 2007; Kim et al., 2008; Settles et al., 2008; Shatkay et al., 2008; Vincze et al., 2008; Nawaz et al., 2010), medicine (Uzuner et al., 2009), news media (Saurí and Pustejovsky, 2009; Wilson, 2008; Rubin et al., 2005; Rubin, 2010), encyclopedia (Ganter and Strube, 2009; Farkas et al., 2010; Szarvas et al., 2012), reviews (Konstantinova et al., 2012; Cruz Díaz, 2013) and social media (Wei et al., 2013).

Although most of the earlier studies experimented with indomain data, there are a few approaches that investigated domain differences. For instance, Szarvas et al. (2012) carried out domain adaptation for biological texts, news media and encyclopedia texts and Vincze (2014) experimented with pieces of news and Wikipedia texts.

Our system described in this paper is also based on supervised machine learning techniques, namely, sequence labeling. The system relies on a rich feature set of lexical, morphological, syntactic, semantic and discourse-based features and also exploits contextual features. To the best of our knowledge, ours is the first system that applies uncertainty detection for Hungarian social media texts.

Besides automatic uncertainty recognition, several studies investigated the distribution of uncertainty cues in different domains (Rizomilioti, 2006; Hyland, 1998; Falahati, 2006). Some of their findings revealed that papers belonging to the humanities contain significantly more cues than papers in sciences. Differences among domains also concern vocabulary items as well as the frequency of certain and uncertain usage of particular uncertainty cues. These findings highlight the practical importance of the domain adaptation of uncertainty detectors.

## 3 Experiments

In this section, we present our methodology to detect uncertainty cues in Hungarian social media texts. We first describe the corpora used together with the uncertainty categories applied and report some statistics on the corpus. Then our machine learning approach is presented in detail, together with its rich feature set.

### 3.1 Corpora

In this study, we made use of texts from two social media sources (Vincze et al., 2014). In the first phase of data preparation, we randomly collected, filtered and cleaned texts from Hungarian social media sites. On the one hand, public Facebook posts and comments were collected and on the other hand, questions and answers from a Hungarian FAQ portal[1] were also collected. This latter source of data was employed as it is supposed to be an authentic resource of the language use of young people in Hungary. The Facebook subcorpus of the data contains 1208 sentences and 8615 tokens whereas the FAQ subcorpus contains 728 sentences and 9702 tokens. Altogether, it makes up 1936 sentences and 18,317 tokens.

Although social media texts are written, their nature is rather similar to oral communication. Speed dominates this kind of communication, causing a number of possibilities for error. Quick typing leads to typos, abbreviations and lack of capitalization, punctuation and accentuated letters in these texts. Accentuated and unaccentuated vowels represent different sounds in Hungarian that can change the meaning of words (compare *szél* "wind" and *szel* "cut"), which may lead to ambiguities. Other types of linguistic creativity are also common, such as the use of smileys and English words and abbreviations in Hungarian texts. These characteristics should be considered when processing Hungarian social media texts.

In the second phase of data preparation, sentences were manually annotated for uncertainty cues (Vincze et al., 2014). Here we just provide a brief summary of uncertainty categories, for a more elaborated version, please refer to Szarvas et al. (2012) and Vincze (2013).

There are several different linguistic phenomena that are categorized as semantic uncertainty. A proposition is **epistemically** uncertain if its truth value cannot be determined on the basis of world knowledge or on the basis of the speaker's current mental state, e.g. *Steve may have failed at the exam.* **Conditionals** (*If it rains, we won't go to the party*) and **investigations** also belong to semantic uncertainty – the latter is especially frequent in research papers, where it is used to formulate research questions (*Here we aim at investigating whether domain specificities affect our results*). **Doxastic** uncertainty is related to beliefs (*I think Steve failed at the exam*).

Some sentences only become uncertain within the context of the discourse. For instance, the sentence *Many studies claim that the population of Cuba has increased in the past 10 years* does not reveal how many (and which) studies claim that, hence the source of the statement on Cuban population remains unclear. This is a type of **weasel** (Ganter and Strube, 2009). Furthermore, **hedges** blur the exact meaning of some quality/quantity as in *Approximately ten people can be admitted to the company.* Lastly, **peacock** cues express unprovable (or unproven) evaluations, qualifications, understatements and exaggerations like *This was the most gorgeous meal I've ever had in this fascinating restaurant.*

Some examples of uncertain sentences are offered here from the corpus, with the original spelling:

(1) Doxastic uncertainty:

| *ugy* | *érzem* | *a* | *denver* | *ki* | *fog* | *kapni* | *.* |
|---|---|---|---|---|---|---|---|
| so | feel-1SG-OBJ | the | Denver | out | will | lose-INF | . |

I think Denver will lose the game.

(2) Epistemic uncertainty:

| *De* | *nem* | *biztos* | *hogy* | *mindenkinek* | *telik* | *1000Ft* | */* | *fő* | */* | *nap* | *kajára* | *!* |
|---|---|---|---|---|---|---|---|---|---|---|---|---|
| but | not | certain | that | everyone-DAT | afford-3SG | 1000Ft | / | person | / | day | food-SUB | ! |

It is not certain that everyone can afford 1000 Ft per day per person for food.

(3) Condition:

| *Megint* | *egy* | *reklám* | *hogy* | *ha* | *nincs* | *samsung* | *telód* | *nem* | *vagy* |
|---|---|---|---|---|---|---|---|---|---|
| again | an | advertisement | that | if | not.have-3SG | Samsung | phone-2SGPOSS | not | are |

| *ember* | *?* |
|---|---|
| human | ? |

[1]http://www.gyakorikerdesek.hu

Yet another advertisement that says that if you don't have a Samsung mobile, you are not a human?

(4) Weasel:

*Na* *ez* *olyan* *,* *de* *mégis* *más* .
well this such , but still different .
Well this is the same but somehow different.

(5) Hedge:

*Elég* *nagy* *probléma* .
enough big problem .
This is such a big problem.

(6) Peacock:

*legeslegjobb* *vagy* *Magyarorszagon* *!*
good-SUPERSUPERLATIVE are Hungary-SUP !
You are the best in Hungary!

In our experiments, we will also make use of the hUnCertainty corpus, which contains 1,091 randomly selected paragraphs from the Hungarian Wikipedia and 300 pieces of criminal news from a Hungarian news portal (`http://www.hvg.hu`) (Vincze, 2014).

Table 1 reports some statistics on the frequency of uncertainty cues in Hungarian (adapted from Vincze et al. (2014)). The annotation principles of the corpora were the same, hence cue distributions in the three domains are comparable. Based on Vincze et al. (2014), we can conclude that the domain of the texts affects the distribution of uncertainty cues: semantic uncertainty cues and discourse-level uncertainty cues are balanced in the news subcorpus but in the Wikipedia and social media corpora, more than 75% of the cues belong to the discourse-level uncertainty type.

| **Uncertainty cue** | **hUnCertainty Wiki** | | **hUnCertainty news** | | **Social media** | |
|---|---|---|---|---|---|---|
| | # | % | # | % | # | % |
| Epistemic | 439 | 7.8 | 358 | 15.16 | 21 | 4.08 |
| Conditional | 154 | 2.74 | 128 | 5.42 | 59 | 11.47 |
| Doxastic | 315 | 5.6 | 710 | 30.08 | 44 | 8.56 |
| Investigation | 31 | 0.55 | 13 | 0.55 | 1 | 0.19 |
| Semantic total | 939 | 16.69 | 1209 | 51.22 | 125 | 24.3 |
| Peacock | 787 | 14 | 94 | 3.98 | 192 | 37.35 |
| Weasel | 1801 | 32.02 | 258 | 10.93 | 50 | 9.72 |
| Hedge | 2098 | 37.3 | 799 | 33.86 | 147 | 28.59 |
| Discourse-level total | 4686 | 83.3 | 1151 | 48.77 | 389 | 75.6 |
| Total | 5625 | 100 | 2360 | 100 | 514 | 100 |

Table 1: Uncertainty cues in three domains.

The most obvious difference among the corpora is the presence of peacocks: their frequency is much higher in social media than in the other datasets. On the other hand, news tend to contain several instances of doxastic cues and Wikipedia has many weasels. In our experiments, we will demonstrate that such differences may strongly affect the performance of uncertainty detectors.

### 3.2 Machine Learning Methods

In order to automatically identify uncertainty cues, we developed a machine learning method to be discussed below. In our experiments, we used our social media corpus as well as the HunCertainty corpus and morphologically and syntactically parsed them with the help of the toolkit `magyarlanc` (Zsibrita et al., 2013).

On the basis of results reported in earlier literature, sequence labeling proved to be one of the most successful methods on English uncertainty detection (see e.g. (Szarvas et al., 2012)), hence we also relied on a method based on conditional random fields (CRF) (Lafferty et al., 2001) in our experiments. We used the MALLET implementation (McCallum, 2002) of CRF. Our feature set is constructed on the basis of earlier uncertainty detectors for Hungarian (Vincze, 2014), however, we added several new features, namely, discourse related features and social media features, due to the specialties of Hungarian social media texts.

- **Orthographic features:** we investigated whether the word contains punctuation marks, digits, uppercase or lowercase letters, the length of the word, consonant bi- and trigrams.

- **Lexical features:** we automatically collected uncertainty cues from the English corpora (see Section 2) annotated for uncertainty and manually translated these lists into Hungarian. Lists were used as binary features: if the lemma of the given word occurred in one of the lists, the feature was assigned the value *true*, else it was *false*.

- **Morphological features:** for each word, its part of speech and lemma were used as a feature. As Hungarian is a morphologically rich language, modality and mood are morphologically expressed (e.g. in *mehetnénk* go-MOD-COND-1PL "we could go", the suffix *-het* refers to modality and the suffix *-né* refers to conditional). Thus each verb was investigated whether it had a modal suffix and whether it was in the conditional mood. Also, we checked whether its form was first person plural or third person plural as these two latter verbal forms are typical instances of expressing generic phrases or generalizations in Hungarian, which are related to weasels. For each noun, its number (i.e. singular/plural) was marked as a feature. Since indefinite pronouns like *valaki* "someone" or *valamilyen* "some" are often used as weasel cues, we checked whether the word was an indefinite pronoun. For each adjective, we marked whether it was comparative or superlative as they can often occur as peacock cues.

- **Syntactic features:** for each word, its dependency label was marked. For each noun, it was checked whether it had a determiner as determinerless nouns may be used as weasels in Hungarian. Hungarian is a pro-drop language, which means that the pronominal subject is not obligatorily present in the clause. Furthermore, a common way to express generalization in Hungarian is to use a third person plural verb without a subject, which is one typical strategy of weasels. Thus, for each verb, it was checked whether it had a subject.

- **Semantic features:** we manually compiled a list of speech act verbs in Hungarian and checked whether the given verb was one of them. Besides, we translated lists of English words with positive and negative content developed for sentiment analysis (Liu, 2012) and checked whether the lemma of the given word occurred in these lists.

- **Discourse related features:** Hungarian is a discourse configurational language, which means that word order is determined by the information structure of the sentence. For instance, the preverbal (focus) position is preserved for the most important (novel) information within the sentence. Thus, for each word we noted its position within the sentence, its relative position to the verb and whether it occurred in the focus position.

- **Social media features:** In Hungarian, accentuated letters denote different phonemes, which might have an effect on word meaning as mentioned above. However, users tend to write without using accents in social media, so in order to simulate this scenario, we removed all accents from the texts and also from the lists applied as lexical features. Smileys and character runs are also typical of social media texts, thus they were marked as features if the word contained or consisted of one.

As contextual features for each word, we applied as features the POS tags and dependency labels of words within a window of size two.

Based on this feature set, we carried out our experiments. It should be mentioned that, as there was only 1 investigation cue in the social media corpus, we neglected this class in our experiments due to sparseness problems.

As our main goal was to see how domain differences affect the efficiency of uncertainty detection, we experimented with several methods. First, we applied ten-fold cross validation on the social media corpus in order to check how a small amount of in-domain data can be exploited in uncertainty detection. Since we had the corpus hUnCertainty at hand, we also made use of cross-domain settings, where hUnCertainty was used as the training database but the evaluation was performed on the social media domain.

We also experimented with very simple domain adaptation techniques. We divided our social media corpus into a training and a test part, in a ratio of 80:20 and first trained our system on these splits. Later, we trained the system on hUnCertainty and evaluated it on the test split of the social media corpus. Lastly, we added the training split of the social media corpus to hUnCertainty and retrained the system with this additional in-domain set of texts. Evaluation was again carried out on the test split of social media texts.

For evaluation, we used the metrics precision, recall and F-score for each class and we also calculated a micro F-score to evaluate the performance of the system as a whole. The results of our experiments will be presented in Section 4.

## 4 Results

The first column of Table 2 represents the results of our in-domain experiments. It is revealed that doxastic cues can be relatively easily identified in social media text, even if only a small dataset is at our disposal. However, the detection of weasels is unsuccessful.

| | **In-domain** | | | **Cross-domain** | | | **Difference** | | |
|---|---|---|---|---|---|---|---|---|---|
| Cue | Recall | Precision | F-score | Recall | Precision | F-score | Recall | Precision | F-score |
| epistemic | 6.52 | 60.00 | 11.76 | 4.35 | 18.18 | 7.02 | -2.17 | -41.82 | -4.75 |
| condition | 8.54 | 21.88 | 12.28 | 29.27 | 36.36 | 32.43 | 20.73 | 14.49 | 20.15 |
| doxastic | 50.56 | 78.95 | 61.64 | 11.24 | 76.92 | 19.61 | -39.33 | -2.02 | -42.04 |
| peacock | 7.41 | 25.64 | 11.49 | 0.74 | 12.50 | 1.40 | -6.67 | -13.14 | -10.10 |
| weasel | 0.00 | 0.00 | 0.00 | 9.26 | 14.71 | 11.36 | 9.26 | 14.71 | 11.36 |
| hedge | 10.80 | 47.50 | 17.59 | 19.89 | 40.23 | 26.62 | 9.09 | -7.27 | 9.02 |
| Micro F | 14.43 | 48.55 | 22.25 | 13.23 | 35.16 | 19.23 | -1.20 | -13.39 | -3.02 |

Table 2: In-domain and cross-domain results on social media texts.

The results of our cross-domain experiments using the full amount of data from both corpora (i.e. hUnCertainty as training data and social media texts as test data) are presented in the second column of Table 2 and the relative differences to the in-domain results are shown in the third column. It can be seen that domain differences have mixed results on different classes of uncertainty cues. On the one hand, performance on peacocks, epistemic and doxastic cues is decreased while on the other hand, conditional cues, weasels and hedges can benefit from the out-domain data. All of this might suggest that different types of linguistic uncertainty behave differently in cross-domain context.

The results of our domain adaptation experiments are reported in Table 3 and the relative differences for in-domain, cross-domain and domain adaptation experiments are shown in Table 4. We can see that domain adaptation could outperform simple cross-domain experiments in the case of all of the uncertainty cue types, especially for epistemic and doxastic cues. However, for doxastic cues and peacocks, it can be observed that out-domain data just harmed performance as compared with the in-domain setting while for all the other cue types, out-domain data could improve the results.

| Cue | SM 80 → SM 20 Recall | Precision | F-score | hUnCertainty → SM 20 Recall | Precision | F-score | hUnCertainty+SM 80 → SM 20 Recall | Precision | F-score |
|---|---|---|---|---|---|---|---|---|---|
| epistemic | 0 | 0 | 0 | 11.11 | 100 | 20 | 22.22 | 100 | 36.36 |
| condition | 10 | 25 | 14.29 | 40 | 26.67 | 32 | 40 | 33.33 | 36.36 |
| doxastic | 68.18 | 88.24 | 76.92 | 9.09 | 100 | 16.67 | 63.64 | 93.33 | 75.68 |
| peacock | 3.45 | 16.67 | 5.71 | 0 | 0 | 0 | 3.45 | 33.33 | 6.25 |
| weasel | 0 | 0 | 0 | 28.57 | 28.57 | 28.57 | 28.57 | 33.33 | 30.77 |
| hedge | 20 | 77.78 | 31.82 | 28.57 | 45.45 | 35.09 | 31.43 | 52.38 | 39.29 |
| Micro F | 21.43 | 64.86 | 32.21 | 16.96 | 39.58 | 23.75 | 30.36 | 57.63 | 39.77 |

Table 3: Results of in-domain, cross-domain and domain adaptation experiments.

| Cue | Cross-domain vs. in-domain Recall | Precision | F-score | DA vs. in-domain Recall | Precision | F-score | Cross-domain vs. DA Recall | Precision | F-score |
|---|---|---|---|---|---|---|---|---|---|
| epistemic | 11.11 | 100 | 20 | 22.22 | 100 | 36.36 | 11.11 | 0 | 16.36 |
| condition | 30 | 1.67 | 17.71 | 30 | 8.33 | 22.07 | 0 | 6.66 | 4.36 |
| doxastic | -59.09 | 11.76 | -60.25 | -4.54 | 5.09 | -1.24 | 54.55 | -6.67 | 59.01 |
| peacock | -3.45 | -16.67 | -5.71 | 0 | 16.66 | 0.54 | 3.45 | 33.33 | 6.25 |
| weasel | 28.57 | 28.57 | 28.57 | 28.57 | 33.33 | 30.77 | 0 | 4.76 | 2.2 |
| hedge | 8.57 | -32.33 | 3.27 | 11.43 | -25.4 | 7.47 | 2.86 | 6.93 | 4.2 |
| Micro F | -4.47 | -25.28 | -8.46 | 8.93 | -7.23 | 7.56 | 13.4 | 18.05 | 16.02 |

Table 4: Differences of performance in cross-domain and domain adaptation settings, compared to in-domain settings.

Figure 1 visualizes our cross-domain and domain adaptation results in terms of F-score, as compared to those achieved in the 80:20 in-domain setting.

## 5 Discussion

Here we experimented with two datasets: one including standard Hungarian texts (approximately 15K sentences) and one including social media texts (less than 2000 sentences). Our results indicated that there are domain differences among social media texts and standard Hungarian texts as uncertainty detection is concerned. Numerical results of cross-domain experiments were in all cases significantly outperformed by domain adaptation (t-test, p = 0.0434), hence even a small amount of in-domain data, that is, annotated social media texts (i.e. about 1600 sentences) can be exploited in uncertainty detection across domains. On the other hand, there is a significant difference in between results obtained in the 80:20 split settings and in the domain adaptation setting (t-test, p = 0.0198), which indicates that a larger amount of out-domain data can also contribute to better results. Thus, the best results can be achieved on social media texts in a scenario when a large amount of out-domain annotated data and a small amount of annotated in-domain data are jointly used as the training dataset.

Comparing the results of in-domain and cross-domain settings, we can observe that in the 80:20 training/test set scenario, epistemic cues and weasel cues cannot be identified at all, which might be related to the fact that these cues rarely occur in the social media data. However, in hUnCertainty, there are quite a few occurrences of them, hence out-domain data may help in their identification, even in a cross-domain setting.

In addition, more interesting differences can be found if uncertainty classes are contrasted. In the case of peacocks, doxastic cues and epistemic cues, cross-domain experiments clearly harm performance with regard to the in-domain settings, despite the much bigger training data. In the domain adaptation setting, however, the added value of in-domain data is noticeable, which indicates that these types of

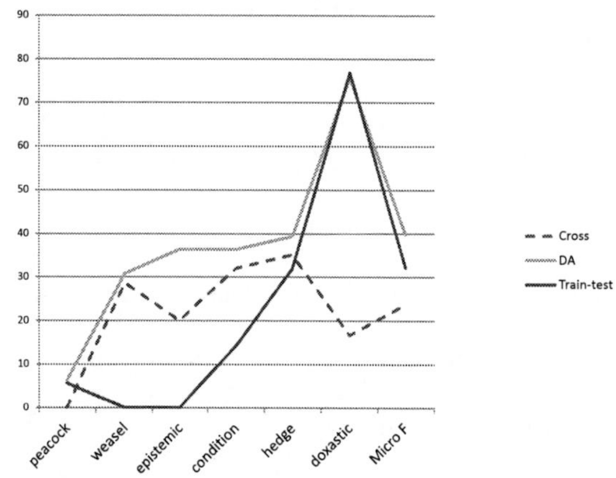


Figure 1: In-domain (Train-test), cross-domain and domain adaptation (DA) results per uncertainty class.

linguistic uncertainty are strongly domain-specific. In other words, the linguistic means to express them may change from domain to domain. For instance, the abbreviated form of *szerintem* "I think", *sztem* is very often used in social media texts as a doxastic cue but it is never used in its short form in standard texts. Thus, adding in-domain data to the training set might provide examples of such cases typical of social media language use. Also, it should be noted that precision values are relatively high for doxastic and epistemic cues even in the cross-domain settings. This might be related to the fact that these types of uncertainty cues occur rarely in social media texts and even if they occur, they are mostly different from the linguistic means used in standard texts. So, the system is unable to identify many of such cues based on the training data but when it marks one cue as doxastic/epistemic, it is most probably a true positive.

In contrast, condition cues, weasels and hedges seem to be less domain-specific according to the results: in-domain data also contributes positively to their identification but only to a moderate degree as compared to doxastic cues for instance (see the gaps in between cross-domain and domain adaptation results in Figure 1). Thus, social media users appear to exploit the same set of linguistic tools to express these types of linguistic uncertainty: the conditional mood is mostly used for conditions, indefinite pronouns are used for weasels, and intensifiers for hedges. We should also note, however, that weasels seem to be very difficult to learn only from social media data, which might be related to data sparsity.

The class of peacocks proved to be the most difficult one to detect in our experiment. There might be several reasons for that. First, this is the class which contained the most occurrences of uncertainty cues in social media, and also, this class is very diverse: it contained a lot of different cues with a low number of average occurrences. Thus, data sparsity might have hindered the performance of the system. Second, the usage of peacock cues seem to depend on the domain to a high extent. For instance, some standard expressions are used in their abbreviated forms like *sajna* instead of *sajnos* "unfortunately". Moreover, some vulgar expressions also occur as peacocks in social media like *szar* "shit", which again cannot be found in standard texts, i.e. Wikipedia and news portals. On the other hand, character runs were especially frequent with peacock cues (like *isteniiiii* instead of *isteni* "heavenly"), which may have also decreased the results. Finally, social media users tend to apply a lot of diminutive forms as peacock, even in the form of neologisms, which again are not easy to detect on the basis of the training data, e.g. *fini* and *fincsi* both occurred as diminutive forms of *finom* "fine, tasty".

Our results can also be contrasted to those obtained on standard Hungarian texts reported in Vincze (2014). The micro F-score interpreted for all uncertainty categories was 44.87. Here, our results are somewhat lower (a micro F-score of 39.77 after domain adaptation) but we should mention that processing social media texts is generally considered to be harder than processing standard texts and we had only a small amount of annotated data at our disposal. Also, it is interesting to note that comparing types of uncertainty cues, numerical results achieved on doxastic cues are higher than those achieved on standard corpora in the in-domain setting (F-scores of 61.64 and 49.15, respectively), which might be explained by the fact that the set of lexical items used as doxastic cues is rather limited in social media whereas in standard texts, there is a greater variety of such cues at the lexical level.

Some of our results suggest that a generalized treatment for all types of linguistic uncertainty classes may not be always viable. This is especially true for peacocks: performance on this class was constantly low, independently of the setting and training dataset we made use of. It seems that the treatment of peacocks require a more refined identification strategy, which might include enhancing the system with extended lists of sentiment words (as peacock cues are closely related to sentiment expressions), morphological analysis of diminutives and more sophisticated ways of processing neologisms and typos. Creating specific methods for the identification of such cues might be a possible direction for future research on uncertainty detection in the social media.

## 6 Conclusions

In this paper, we presented our system for identifying uncertainty cues in Hungarian social media texts. For this purpose, we created a machine learning based uncertainty detector which was based on a rich features set including lexical, morphological, syntactic, semantic and discourse-based features. Our system was evaluated on a small set of manually annotated social media texts. In order to see how domain differences affect machine learning, we also performed cross-domain and domain adaptation experiments using an annotated corpus of standard Hungarian texts. Our results indicated that specialties of social media texts should be accounted for when implementing an uncertainty detector. Also, selecting the training data has a significant effect on learning efficiency, but adding out-domain data to a small set of in-domain data can also contribute to performance. Moreover, differences among uncertainty cue types may also affect the efficiency of uncertainty detection and therefore some types of linguistic uncertainty may require special treatment in uncertainty detection.

In the future, we would like to improve our system by adding more refined techniques for processing Hungarian social media texts. We also intend to experiment with peacocks in more detail, which proved to be the most difficult uncertainty class to detect. Finally, as the majority of studies on uncertainty detection focus on English, it would be interesting to see how our system could perform on social media texts written in English. In this way, interlingual comparisons could also be made, which can be beneficial for both linguistics and natural language processing.

## References

Wendy W. Chapman, David Chu, and John N. Dowling. 2007. Context: An algorithm for identifying contextual features from clinical text. In *Proceedings of the ACL Workshop on BioNLP 2007*, pages 81–88.

David Clausen. 2010. HedgeHunter: a system for hedge detection and uncertainty classification. In *Proceedings of the Fourteenth Conference on Computational Natural Language Learning — Shared Task*, CoNLL '10: Shared Task, pages 120–125, Uppsala, Sweden. Association for Computational Linguistics.

Noa P. Cruz Díaz. 2013. Detecting negated and uncertain information in biomedical and review texts. In *Proceedings of the Student Research Workshop associated with RANLP 2013*, pages 45–50, Hissar, Bulgaria, September. RANLP 2013 Organising Committee.

Reza Falahati. 2006. The use of hedging across different disciplines and rhetorical sections of research articles. In Nicole Carter, Loreley Hadic-Zabala, Anne Rimrott, and Dennis Ryan Storoshenko, editors, *Proceedings of the 22nd NorthWest Linguistics Conference (NWLC22)*, pages 99–112, Burnaby, Canada. Simon Fraser University.

Richárd Farkas, Veronika Vincze, György Móra, János Csirik, and György Szarvas. 2010. The CoNLL-2010 Shared Task: Learning to Detect Hedges and their Scope in Natural Language Text. In *Proceedings of the Fourteenth Conference on Computational Natural Language Learning (CoNLL-2010): Shared Task*, pages 1–12, Uppsala, Sweden, July. Association for Computational Linguistics.

Eraldo R. Fernandes, Carlos E. M. Crestana, and Ruy L. Milidiú. 2010. Hedge detection using the RelHunter approach. In *Proceedings of the Fourteenth Conference on Computational Natural Language Learning — Shared Task*, CoNLL '10: Shared Task, pages 64–69, Uppsala, Sweden. Association for Computational Linguistics.

Viola Ganter and Michael Strube. 2009. Finding Hedges by Chasing Weasels: Hedge Detection Using Wikipedia Tags and Shallow Linguistic Features. In *Proceedings of the ACL-IJCNLP 2009 Conference Short Papers*, pages 173–176, Suntec, Singapore, August. Association for Computational Linguistics.

Ken Hyland. 1998. Boosters, hedging and the negotiation of academic knowledge. *Text*, 18(3):349–382.

Jin-Dong Kim, Tomoko Ohta, and Jun'ichi Tsujii. 2008. Corpus annotation for mining biomedical events from literature. *BMC Bioinformatics*, 9(Suppl 10).

Natalia Konstantinova, Sheila C.M. de Sousa, Noa P. Cruz, Manuel J. Mana, Maite Taboada, and Ruslan Mitkov. 2012. A review corpus annotated for negation, speculation and their scope. In Nicoletta Calzolari (Conference Chair), Khalid Choukri, Thierry Declerck, Mehmet Ugur Dogan, Bente Maegaard, Joseph Mariani, Jan Odijk, and Stelios Piperidis, editors, *Proceedings of the Eight International Conference on Language Resources and Evaluation (LREC'12)*, Istanbul, Turkey, may. European Language Resources Association (ELRA).

John Lafferty, Andrew McCallum, and Fernando Pereira. 2001. Conditional random fields: Probabilistic models for segmenting and labeling sequence data. In *Proceedings of ICML-01, 18th Int. Conf. on Machine Learning*, pages 282–289. Morgan Kaufmann.

Xinxin Li, Jianping Shen, Xiang Gao, and Xuan Wang. 2010. Exploiting rich features for detecting hedges and their scope. In *Proceedings of the Fourteenth Conference on Computational Natural Language Learning — Shared Task*, CoNLL '10: Shared Task, pages 78–83, Uppsala, Sweden. Association for Computational Linguistics.

Marc Light, Xin Ying Qiu, and Padmini Srinivasan. 2004. The language of bioscience: Facts, speculations, and statements in between. In *Proc. of the HLT-NAACL 2004 Workshop: Biolink 2004, Linking Biological Literature, Ontologies and Databases*, pages 17–24.

Bing Liu. 2012. *Sentiment Analysis and Opinion Mining*. Morgan & Claypool Publishers.

Andrew Kachites McCallum. 2002. *MALLET: A Machine Learning for Language Toolkit*. http://mallet.cs.umass.edu.

Ben Medlock and Ted Briscoe. 2007. Weakly Supervised Learning for Hedge Classification in Scientific Literature. In *Proceedings of the ACL*, pages 992–999, Prague, Czech Republic, June.

Roser Morante and Walter Daelemans. 2009. Learning the scope of hedge cues in biomedical texts. In *Proceedings of the BioNLP 2009 Workshop*, pages 28–36, Boulder, Colorado, June. Association for Computational Linguistics.

Roser Morante and Caroline Sporleder. 2012. Modality and negation: An introduction to the special issue. *Computational Linguistics*, 38:223–260, June.

Raheel Nawaz, Paul Thompson, and Sophia Ananiadou. 2010. Evaluating a meta-knowledge annotation scheme for bio-events. In *Proceedings of the Workshop on Negation and Speculation in Natural Language Processing*, pages 69–77, Uppsala, Sweden, July. University of Antwerp.

Arzucan Özgür and Dragomir R. Radev. 2009. Detecting speculations and their scopes in scientific text. In *Proceedings of the 2009 Conference on Empirical Methods in Natural Language Processing*, pages 1398–1407, Singapore, August. Association for Computational Linguistics.

Marek Rei and Ted Briscoe. 2010. Combining manual rules and supervised learning for hedge cue and scope detection. In *Proceedings of the Fourteenth Conference on Computational Natural Language Learning — Shared Task*, CoNLL '10: Shared Task, pages 56–63, Uppsala, Sweden. Association for Computational Linguistics.

Vassiliki Rizomilioti. 2006. Exploring epistemic modality in academic discourse using corpora. In Elisabet Arnó Macia, Antonia Soler Cervera, and Carmen Rueda Ramos, editors, *Information Technology in Languages for Specific Purposes*, volume 7 of *Educational Linguistics*, pages 53–71. Springer US.

Victoria L. Rubin, Elizabeth D. Liddy, and Noriko Kando. 2005. Certainty identification in texts: Categorization model and manual tagging results. In J.G. Shanahan, J. Qu, and J. Wiebe, editors, *Computing attitude and affect in text: Theory and applications (the information retrieval series)*, New York. Springer Verlag.

Victoria L. Rubin. 2010. Epistemic modality: From uncertainty to certainty in the context of information seeking as interactions with texts. *Information Processing & Management*, 46(5):533–540.

Liliana Mamani Sánchez, Baoli Li, and Carl Vogel. 2010. Exploiting ccg structures with tree kernels for speculation detection. In *Proceedings of the Fourteenth Conference on Computational Natural Language Learning — Shared Task*, CoNLL '10: Shared Task, pages 126–131, Uppsala, Sweden. Association for Computational Linguistics.

Roser Saurí and James Pustejovsky. 2009. FactBank: a corpus annotated with event factuality. *Language Resources and Evaluation*, 43:227–268.

Burr Settles, Mark Craven, and Lewis Friedland. 2008. Active learning with real annotation costs. In *Proceedings of the NIPS Workshop on Cost-Sensitive Learning*, pages 1–10.

Hagit Shatkay, Fengxia Pan, Andrey Rzhetsky, and W. John Wilbur. 2008. Multi-dimensional classification of biomedical text: Toward automated, practical provision of high-utility text to diverse users. *Bioinformatics*, 24(18):2086–2093.

György Szarvas, Veronika Vincze, Richárd Farkas, György Móra, and Iryna Gurevych. 2012. Cross-genre and cross-domain detection of semantic uncertainty. *Computational Linguistics*, 38:335–367, June.

Buzhou Tang, Xiaolong Wang, Xuan Wang, Bo Yuan, and Shixi Fan. 2010. A cascade method for detecting hedges and their scope in natural language text. In *Proceedings of the Fourteenth Conference on Computational Natural Language Learning — Shared Task*, CoNLL '10: Shared Task, pages 13–17, Uppsala, Sweden. Association for Computational Linguistics.

Özlem Uzuner, Xiaoran Zhang, and Tawanda Sibanda. 2009. Machine Learning and Rule-based Approaches to Assertion Classification. *Journal of the American Medical Informatics Association*, 16(1):109–115, January.

Erik Velldal. 2010. Detecting uncertainty in biomedical literature: A simple disambiguation approach using sparse random indexing. In *Proceedings of SMBM 2010*, pages 75–83, Cambridge, UK.

Veronika Vincze, György Szarvas, Richárd Farkas, György Móra, and János Csirik. 2008. The BioScope Corpus: Biomedical Texts Annotated for Uncertainty, Negation and their Scopes. *BMC Bioinformatics*, 9(Suppl 11):S9.

Veronika Vincze, Katalin Ilona Simkó, and Viktor Varga. 2014. Annotating uncertainty in hungarian webtext. In *Proceedings of LAW VIII - The 8th Linguistic Annotation Workshop*, pages 64–69, Dublin, Ireland, August. Association for Computational Linguistics and Dublin City University.

Veronika Vincze. 2013. Weasels, Hedges and Peacocks: Discourse-level Uncertainty in Wikipedia Articles. In *Proceedings of the Sixth International Joint Conference on Natural Language Processing*, pages 383–391, Nagoya, Japan, October. Asian Federation of Natural Language Processing.

Veronika Vincze. 2014. Uncertainty detection in Hungarian texts. In *Proceedings of Coling 2014*.

Zhongyu Wei, Junwen Chen, Wei Gao, Binyang Li, Lanjun Zhou, Yulan He, and Kam-Fai Wong. 2013. An empirical study on uncertainty identification in social media context. In *Proceedings of the 51st Annual Meeting of the Association for Computational Linguistics (Volume 2: Short Papers)*, pages 58–62, Sofia, Bulgaria, August. Association for Computational Linguistics.

Theresa Ann Wilson. 2008. *Fine-grained Subjectivity and Sentiment Analysis: Recognizing the Intensity, Polarity, and Attitudes of Private States*. Ph.D. thesis, University of Pittsburgh, Pittsburgh.

Shaodian Zhang, Hai Zhao, Guodong Zhou, and Bao-Liang Lu. 2010. Hedge detection and scope finding by sequence labeling with normalized feature selection. In *Proceedings of the Fourteenth Conference on Computational Natural Language Learning — Shared Task*, CoNLL '10: Shared Task, pages 92–99, Uppsala, Sweden. Association for Computational Linguistics.

János Zsibrita, Veronika Vincze, and Richárd Farkas. 2013. magyarlanc: A Toolkit for Morphological and Dependency Parsing of Hungarian. In *Proceedings of RANLP-2013*, pages 763–771, Hissar, Bulgaria.

# Detecting Level of Belief in Chinese and Spanish

**Juan Pablo Colomer**
Columbia University
j.p.colomer@columbia.edu

**Keyu Lai**
Columbia University
kl2844@columbia.edu

**Owen Rambow**
CCLS
Columbia University
rambow@ccls.columbia.edu

## Abstract

There has been extensive work on detecting the level of committed belief (also known as "factuality") that an author is expressing towards the propositions in his or her utterances. Previous work on English has revealed that this can be done as a word tagging task. In this paper, we investigate the same task for Chinese and Spanish, two very different languages from English and from each other.

## 1 Introduction: Committed Belief

The term "committed belief" (Diab et al., 2009) has been used to refer to the commitment of a writer towards the propositions she communicates: does she fully believe the proposition, does she believe the proposition may be true, is she reporting someone else's belief without commenting on it, or is she reporting something other than a belief, namely a hope or desire? The notion is closely related to "factuality", which Saurí and Pustejovsky (2009) define as the communicative intention of the writer to make the reader believe what her beliefs are. For a fuller discussion of the relation between the two notions and related notions such as factivity and modality, see (Prabhakaran et al., 2015).

Determining the writer's degree of commitment to the propositions in her text is crucial in understanding text, since if an NLP system fails to identify a proposition as merely wished as opposed to asserted, then clearly the NLP system is failing to understand what is being communicated.

While work on English has been available (both for Committed Belief and for Factuality), no resources have been available for other languages. Recently, the Linguistic Data Consortium (LDC) has annotated small corpora for Chinese and Spanish. This paper summarizes initial systems trained on these corpora.

## 2 Data

The LDC has released one data set each for Chinese and Spanish committed belief word tagging to the research groups participating in the DARPA DEFT program.[1] The LDC will make this data available to the general research community. We describe these data sets in this section.

### 2.1 Annotation Scheme

The annotation is a word-based annotation. The goal of the annotation is to identify propositions in the text and to tag them with the degree of Committed Belief. This degree is tagged on the word which is the syntactic head of the proposition. For such syntactic heads, 4 tags are available, they are summarized in Table 1. All words which are not the syntactic heads of propositions get a default "O" tag (or "Other"). We only evaluate our performance on the four belief tags.

This annotation scheme extends the annotation scheme proposed by Diab et al. (2009) by splitting its NCB tag into NCB and ROB. (In the scheme of (Diab et al., 2009), our NCB and ROB were combined because in both tags we cannot infer a committed belief of the writer; however, in terms of our knowledge of the writer's cognitive state, they clearly represent very different categories.) For a fuller discussion of the tagsets, see (Werner et al., 2015).

[1] LDC2015E99 for Chinese and LDC2016E40 for Spanish.



*Proceedings of the Workshop on Extra-Propositional Aspects of Meaning in Computational Linguistics*, pages 22–30, Osaka, Japan, December 12 2016.

| Tag | Meaning | Example |
|---|---|---|
| CB | Committed Belief | John will arrive tomorrow |
| NCB | Non-committed Belief | John may arrive tomorrow |
| ROB | Reported Belief | Mary says that John will arrive tomorrow |
| NA | Not a Belief | I hope that John will arrive tomorrow |

Table 1: Explanation of the four belief tags used in the annotation, along with English examples

### 2.2 Chinese Data

The Chinese corpus is sampled from Chinese Discussion forums. The topics mostly focus on politics and news stories. The corpus is annotated at the character level, not the word level. To annotate what would be considered a word, the corpus uses the label of the first annotated character as the label for the whole word. For example, if the word 访问'access' is the head of a proposition in which the author expresses committed belief, then the annotation is "访/CB问/O" rather than "访问/CB". The character 访is annotated as CB rather than the word 访问because the Committed Belief annotation did not want to have to perform word segmentation as part of the annotation task, which can be a time consuming (and not always obvious) task. As a result, the annotation scheme is compatible with different choices as to word segmentation.

We do perform word segmentation in this work, using the Stanford tools (Manning et al., 2014). When we do word segmentation, and if at least one character has an annotation, then that annotation is carried over to the whole word. If all characters comprised by the word don't have annotations, then the word remains unlabelled (i.e., it gets the O tag). It did not happen in our corpus that more than one character in the same word received tags which were contradictory. We compare using characters and using words in Section 4.1.

We divided the whole corpus into 80% training set, 10% development set and 10% test set in term of characters for further experiment. The numbers of characters in each subsets are: training set: 96735; development set: 11747; test set: 12155. Here is a simple example:

(1) 妈妈 说/CB 我 看/ROB 他 喜欢/ROB 吃 这个
Mom say I think he like eat this
'Mom said I think he likes eating this'

| | Training | Development | Test | Training | Development | Test |
|---|---|---|---|---|---|---|
| | Chinese | | | Spanish | | |
| CB | 7,939 (13%) | 974 (14%) | 1,076 (15%) | 4,563 (7%) | 496 (7%) | 600 (7%) |
| NA | 5,294 (9%) | 639 (9%) | 492 (7%) | 3,288 (5%) | 406 (6%) | 494 (6%) |
| NCB | 209 (0%) | 39 (1%) | 24 (0%) | 267 (0%) | 32 (0%) | 46 (1%) |
| ROB | 1,086 (0%) | 72 (1%) | 57 (1%) | 437 (1%) | 13 (0%) | 47 (1%) |
| O | 44,406 (75%) | 5,432 (76%) | 5,621 (77%) | 55,215 (87%) | 6,228 (86%) | 7,448 (86%) |
| Total | 58,934 | 7,156 | 7,270 | 63,770 | 7,175 | 8,635 |

Table 2: Chinese and Spanish words per label and data set

### 2.3 Spanish Data

The Spanish corpus was also extracted from discussion forums. It is important to note that people from different Spanish speaking countries write in these forums. Also, they tend to use an informal language, thus there is a significant diversity of slang words which makes the task hard even for a Spanish native speaker.

The corpus was separated approximately into 80% training set, 10% development set and 10% test set in terms of labeled words.

Example:

(2) Creo/CB que debería/NCB haberlo escrito/CB en mayúscula
think that should have-it written in uppercase
'I think I should have written it in capital letters'

### 2.4 Discussion of Data Sets

The data sets are summarized in Table 2. Several observations are in order:

- For each languages, the distribution of the labels is fairly similar in the training, development, and test sets.
- In Spanish, fewer words are tagged with belief labels (i.e., more words are tagged with O). This is because Spanish has determiners, auxiliaries, and in general more function words which do not receive Committed Belief labels.
- In both languages, there are very few NCB and ROB tags (with ROB more frequent than NCB). As we will see, these tags are accordingly hard to predict.

Since the information about Committed Belief is expressed as tags on words, we can define the task as a word-tagging task, as was also done previously for English.

## 3 Features and Experimental Setup

### 3.1 Features Used in Both Languages

In our analysis we used some common features for both languages. These features are the following:

- Word: One-hot encoding representation.
- Part-of-Speech (POS): One-hot encoding representation (using different tagsets for the two languages of course). The use of POS is motivated by the need to find the syntactic heads of propositions, which are typically verbs.
- 64 dimension word embedding: We used Polyglot (Al-Rfou et al., 2013) to get the word embedding for the two languages.

For word segmentation in Chinese and POS-tagging in Chinese and Spanish, we used the Stanford tools (Manning et al., 2014).

Additionally, the process to obtain the features vector of a word is the same on Chinese and Spanish. We experimented with 3 configurations of context windows to compute above features; they differ in where in the 5-word context window the target word is found. Let $w_0$ be the target word and $w_i$ the word in $i$-th position relative to $w_0$.

- [-2/+2]: $[w_{-2}, w_{-1}, w_0, w_1, w_2]$
- [-3/+1]: $[w_{-3}, w_{-2}, w_{-1}, w_0, w_1]$
- [-4/0]: $[w_{-4}, w_{-3}, w_{-2}, w_{-1}, w_0]$

Thus, the feature vector of the target word is formed by stacking the features' representations of all words in the context window.

### 3.2 Features Used only in Spanish

In addition to the features described in 3.1 an important feature for Spanish is the lemma of a word. The software used to extract these features is Freeling 3.0 (Padró and Stanilovsky, 2012).

### 3.3 Baseline

We will consider our baseline to be a system that trains only on words and uses the [-2,+2] context window (i.e., the words are chosen to be centered on the context word). We also consider this our baseline for Chinese, even though it requires the additional step of word segmentation. This is because a character-based model performs much worse, as we will see in Sectionsec:ch-ch-w.

### 3.4 Experimental Setup

For both languages, we trained and fine-tuned the parameters of a Linear SVM classifiers from Scikit-learn library (Pedregosa et al., 2011). This classifier implements a one-vs-all strategy which has a similar performance as an SVM classifier with one-vs-one strategy, but its runtime is considerably faster.

We report results only on the tags for the heads of propositions (i.e., not on the O tag). We use F-measure to report results, and used a weighted average F-measure to summarize the results.

## 4 Chinese Results

### 4.1 Characters or Words?

Chinese is typically written without spaces between two words (different from European languages including Spanish and English). The identification of words in Chinese is a typical initial processing step in Chinese NLP. However, since the annotation is in fact at the character level (see Section 2.2), we perform experiments to see if annotation at the character level performs better than at the word levels. We use two windows for the character experiments, namely [-2,+2] (a five-character window centered on the target character) and [-4,+4] (a nine-character window centered on the target character). For the word experiments, we use the baseline configuration (only words, with a [-2,+2] context window.

The results are shown in Table 3. As can be seen, using words far outperforms characters, even if we use a much larger window for characters than for words. We therefore use words for the remainder of our experiments.

| | Characters [-2/+2] | | | Characters [-4/+4] | | | Words [-2/+2] | | |
|---|---|---|---|---|---|---|---|---|---|
| | prec. | recall | f1 | prec. | recall | f1 | prec. | recall | f1 |
| CB | 0.4008 | 0.4714 | 0.4333 | 0.4406 | 0.4629 | 0.4515 | 0.5533 | 0.5329 | **0.5429** |
| NA | 0.3539 | 0.4059 | 0.3781 | 0.3798 | 0.4088 | 0.3937 | 0.5129 | 0.4351 | **0.4708** |
| NCB | 0.0353 | 0.1429 | 0.0566 | 0.0567 | 0.1905 | 0.0874 | 0.0968 | 0.2308 | **0.1364** |
| ROB | 0.0349 | 0.1579 | 0.0571 | 0.0353 | 0.1579 | 0.0577 | 0.0723 | 0.2361 | **0.1107** |
| Wted Avg. | 0.3601 | 0.4266 | 0.3888 | 0.3926 | 0.4240 | 0.4056 | 0.5083 | 0.4772 | **0.4891** |

Table 3: Chinese: Comparison of labeling characters with labeling words (after word segmentation); first six result columns are based on characters with different context windows, next three columns are based on words. Boldface indicates the best F1-measure performance per label across the three experiments.

### 4.2 Adding POS

We now investigate the role of part-of-speech (POS) tags. We first use the same window as in the baseline (the last experiment in Table 3), namely [-2,+2], i.e., the target word and two words to the left and two words to the right. The results for the same window are shown in the first three result columns in Table 4. Comparing to the word results from Table3, we see that the addition of POS increases the results for the common tags CB and NA as well as for ROB by around 2% absolute; NCB is not affected. We therefore keep POS tags in all subsequent experiments.

In a second round of experiments we vary the context window. In the results for [-3,+1], we let the target word be the third word in the 5-word window (middle three result columns in Table 4), and then we consider the [-4,0] window in which the target word is the last word in the 5-word window (last three result columns in Table 4). We see that except for ROB, the best performance is always obtained using a window centered on the target word.

### 4.3 Using Word Embeddings

Finally, we add word embeddings to the word and POS features. We again experiment with the position of the target word in the context window. The results are shown in Table 5. We see that when we use word embeddings, the left context becomes more valuable than the right context, and we now obtain better results if we use context window [-3,+1] (i.e., the target word is in position 4 of the 5-word

| | Words and POS [-2/+2] | | | Words and POS [-3/+1] | | | Words and POS [-4/0] | | |
|---|---|---|---|---|---|---|---|---|---|
| | prec. | recall | f1 | prec. | recall | f1 | prec. | recall | f1 |
| CB | 0.5643 | 0.5719 | **0.5681** | 0.5708 | 0.5585 | 0.5646 | 0.5494 | 0.5370 | 0.5431 |
| NA | 0.5273 | 0.4679 | **0.4959** | 0.5083 | 0.4789 | 0.4932 | 0.4903 | 0.4726 | 0.4813 |
| NCB | 0.1000 | 0.2051 | **0.1345** | 0.0964 | 0.2051 | 0.1311 | 0.0882 | 0.2308 | 0.1277 |
| ROB | 0.0872 | 0.2639 | 0.1310 | 0.1005 | 0.3056 | **0.1512** | 0.0756 | 0.2500 | 0.1161 |
| Wted AVG | 0.5206 | 0.5120 | **0.5134** | 0.5175 | 0.5103 | 0.5112 | 0.4976 | 0.4942 | 0.4932 |

Table 4: Chinese: Using POS tags, experimenting with different positions for the target word $w_0$ in the window. Boldface indicates the best F1-measure performance per label across the three experiments.

context window). These results are slightly better for all labels compared to the best results without word embeddings; for ROB, they are only slightly worse.

| | Words, POS, and Embedding [-2/+2] | | | Words, POS, and Embedding [-3/+1] | | |
|---|---|---|---|---|---|---|
| | prec. | recall | f1 | prec. | recall | f1 |
| CB | 0.5518 | 0.5688 | 0.5602 | 0.5647 | 0.5780 | **0.5713** |
| NA | 0.5217 | 0.4898 | 0.5052 | 0.5078 | 0.5086 | **0.5082** |
| NCB | 0.0667 | 0.1282 | 0.0877 | 0.1061 | 0.1795 | **0.1333** |
| ROB | 0.0675 | 0.2222 | 0.1036 | 0.0940 | 0.3056 | **0.1438** |
| Weighted AVG | 0.5100 | 0.5151 | 0.5104 | 0.5139 | 0.5319 | **0.5204** |

Table 5: Chinese: Using word embeddings, with context window [-2,+2] (word in position 3 of 5-word context window, first three result columns) and context window [-3,+1] (word in position 4 of 5-word context window, last three result columns). Boldface indicates the best F1-measure performance per label across the three experiments.

## 5 Spanish Results

### 5.1 Lexical Features

We start out our experiments on the development set by using only lexical features, and we vary the context window. As can be seen from the results in Table 6, the best results for the common labels CB and NA are obtained for context window [-2,+2] (i.e., the target word is centered in the window), while the rarer labels ROB and NCB, performing far worse overall, profit from a greater left context window. The effect is particularly strong for ROB, presumably because the larger left context allows the system to detect verbs of attribution (or perhaps the subordinating conjunction *que* 'that').

| | Words [-2/+2] | | | Words [-3/+1] | | | Words [-4/0] | | |
|---|---|---|---|---|---|---|---|---|---|
| | prec. | recall | f1 | prec. | recall | f1 | prec. | recall | f1 |
| CB | 0.6853 | 0.5444 | **0.6067** | 0.6559 | 0.5343 | 0.5889 | 0.6432 | 0.5343 | 0.5837 |
| NA | 0.6949 | 0.5665 | **0.6242** | 0.6787 | 0.5567 | 0.6116 | 0.6817 | 0.5222 | 0.5914 |
| NCB | 0.3636 | 0.1250 | 0.1860 | 0.3077 | 0.1250 | 0.1778 | 0.4000 | 0.1250 | **0.1905** |
| ROB | 0.0625 | 0.0769 | 0.0690 | 0.0667 | 0.0769 | 0.0714 | 0.1538 | 0.1538 | **0.1538** |
| Wted AVG | 0.6700 | 0.5333 | **0.5926** | 0.6458 | 0.5238 | 0.5776 | 0.6448 | 0.5101 | 0.5678 |

Table 6: Spanish: Word Features. Boldface indicates the best F1-measure performance per label across the three experiments.

### 5.2 Adding POS and Lemmas

In Table 7, we add POS tags as features. We see that results improve across the board. For the common tags CB and NA, the best results continue to be obtained from a the [-2,+2] context window centered on the target word, while ROB and NCB still profit from more left context.

Lemmas can be a way of reducing data sparseness in highly inflected languages, since they collapse all inflected forms of a lexeme to a single representative. Results using words, POS tags, and lemmas are shown in Table 8. We see only relatively small changes resulting from the use of lemmas. For reasons that are not clear to us, the [-3,+1] context window now performs best on average as well as for the specific tags CB, NCB, and ROB. For the NA tag, even more left context is useful, with the [-4,0] context window performing best. When comparing the best results per label to the best results per label without lemmas (Table 7), we see that the use of lemmas increases the performance for all labels except ROB. However, because the best performance with lemmas is achieved using different configurations, the weighted average does not improve through the use of lemmas.

| | Words and POS [-2/+2] | | | Words and POS [-3/+1] | | | Words and POS [-4/0] | | |
|---|---|---|---|---|---|---|---|---|---|
| | prec. | recall | f1 | prec. | recall | f1 | prec. | recall | f1 |
| CB | 0.6681 | 0.6411 | **0.6543** | 0.6542 | 0.6371 | 0.6456 | 0.6475 | 0.6593 | 0.6533 |
| NA | 0.6987 | 0.6798 | **0.6891** | 0.6759 | 0.6576 | 0.6667 | 0.6856 | 0.6552 | 0.6700 |
| NCB | 0.2857 | 0.1250 | 0.1739 | 0.3571 | 0.1563 | **0.2174** | 0.3636 | 0.1250 | 0.1860 |
| ROB | 0.1176 | 0.1538 | 0.1333 | 0.1176 | 0.1538 | 0.1333 | 0.2222 | 0.1538 | **0.1818** |
| Wted AVG | 0.6607 | 0.6336 | **0.6458** | 0.6461 | 0.623 | 0.6331 | 0.6484 | 0.6325 | 0.6382 |

Table 7: Spanish: Using words and POS tags. Boldface indicates the best F1-measure performance per label across the three experiments.

| | Words, POS, Lemma [-2/+2] | | | Words, POS, Lemma [-3/+1] | | | Words, POS, Lemma [-4/0] | | |
|---|---|---|---|---|---|---|---|---|---|
| | prec. | recall | f1 | prec. | recall | f1 | prec. | recall | f1 |
| CB | 0.6762 | 0.6190 | 0.6463 | 0.6716 | 0.6431 | **0.6571** | 0.6522 | 0.6351 | 0.6435 |
| NA | 0.6738 | 0.6970 | 0.6852 | 0.6801 | 0.6650 | 0.6725 | 0.6977 | 0.6823 | **0.6899** |
| NCB | 0.2500 | 0.1250 | 0.1667 | 0.3750 | 0.1875 | **0.2500** | 0.3125 | 0.1563 | 0.2083 |
| ROB | 0.0952 | 0.1538 | 0.1176 | 0.1667 | 0.1538 | **0.1600** | 0.1538 | 0.1538 | 0.1538 |
| Wted AVG | 0.6528 | 0.6294 | 0.6395 | 0.6583 | 0.6304 | **0.6431** | 0.6534 | 0.6326 | 0.6420 |

Table 8: Spanish: Adding Lemmas. Boldface indicates the best F1-measure performance per label across the three experiments.

### 5.3 Using Word Embeddings

We finally add word embeddings (retaining words, POS, and lemmas). The results are shown in Table 9, for the three context windows. We observe that the best window configuration differs even more by label than before, with NA preferring a balanced left and right context.

The best performing single configuration (as measured by weighted average) is [-3,+1], i.e., the target word in the 4th position in the 5-word window, which is also our overall best performing configuration for Spanish.

## 6 Results on Test Sets

We apply the best performing configurations of each language to the respective held-out test sets, with the results shown in Table 10. We see for both languages a decrease compared to the best result on the development set, of 4% absolute for Chinese, and 7% absolute for Spanish. Presumably this is at least partially due to overfitting to the development set.

## 7 Discussion

We have trained belief taggers for Chinese and Spanish. Results on the development sets show striking similarities between the two languages:

| | Words, POS, Lemmas, Embeddings [-2/+2] | | | Words, POS, Lemmas, Embeddings [-3/+1] | | | Words, POS, Lemmas, Embeddings [-4/0] | | |
|---|---|---|---|---|---|---|---|---|---|
| | prec. | recall | f1 | prec. | recall | f1 | prec. | recall | f1 |
| CB | 0.6763 | 0.6149 | 0.6441 | 0.6709 | 0.6452 | 0.6578 | 0.6739 | 0.6472 | **0.6598** |
| NA | 0.6872 | 0.6872 | **0.6872** | 0.6990 | 0.6576 | 0.6777 | 0.6959 | 0.6650 | 0.6801 |
| NCB | 0.3529 | 0.1875 | 0.2449 | 0.4 | 0.25 | **0.3077** | 0.375 | 0.1875 | 0.25 |
| ROB | 0.0909 | 0.1538 | 0.1143 | 0.125 | 0.1538 | **0.1379** | 0.1053 | 0.1538 | 0.125 |
| Wted AVG | 0.6620 | 0.6251 | 0.6430 | 0.6663 | 0.6304 | **0.6474** | 0.6654 | 0.6325 | 0.6473 |

Table 9: Spanish: Using word embeddings. Boldface indicates the best F1-measure performance per label across the three experiments.

Chinese: Test Results for Features: Word, Part-Of-Speech, Word Embedding on context window [-3,+1]

| | precision | recall | f1-score |
|---|---|---|---|
| CB | 0.5581 | 0.5000 | 0.5275 |
| NA | 0.4016 | 0.5142 | 0.4510 |
| NCB | 0.0118 | 0.0417 | 0.0183 |
| ROB | 0.0484 | 0.2105 | 0.0787 |
| Weighted AVG | 0.4858 | 0.4876 | 0.4818 |

Spanish: Test Results for Features: Word, Part-Of-Speech, Lemma, Word Embedding on context window [-3,+1]

| | precision | recall | f1-score |
|---|---|---|---|
| CB | 0.598 | 0.605 | 0.6015 |
| NA | 0.6195 | 0.6559 | 0.6372 |
| NCB | 0.1053 | 0.0435 | 0.0615 |
| ROB | 0.0833 | 0.0426 | 0.0563 |
| Weighted AVG | 0.5675 | 0.5822 | 0.5738 |

Table 10: The results of the best configurations on the test sets

- For both languages, the best configuration includes word, POS, and word embeddings, using context window [-3,+1] (in which the target word in the 4th position of the 5-word context window).
- For both languages, the major increase over using only words comes from POS tags. This is plausible since they help the tagger identify the syntactic heads of propositions (which need to be tagged with a belief tag).
- For both languages, word embeddings help a small amount. The relatively small contribution from the word embeddings may be due to the fact that the word embeddings do not capture the right generalizations for this task, or they are trained on corpora that are too small or not representative of our corpora.
- For both languages, the distribution of the tags is fairly similar, with the result that the rare tags NCB and ROB are predicted badly.
- The use of lemmas for Spanish does not contribute much.

There are also some interesting differences between the languages.

- For each tag, the Chinese results are inferior to the Spanish results, except tag ROB. We have no explanation for the fact that ROB performs better in Chinese than in Spanish.
- The differences in performance between Chinese and Spanish are particularly large (in relative terms) for NA and NCB. These are two types of belief which in Spanish are often signaled in the inflections. For example, NAs are often signaled by infinitives which are complements of verbs of obligation (*tiene que transofrmarla*) or wishing (*quiere sostener*), and NCBs are signaled by infinitives after modal verbs (*debe sentir*).

(3) a. tiene/CB que transformarla/NA si quiere/NA sostener/NA el negocio
must transform-it if desires sustain the business
'He must transform it if he wants to sustain business'

b. uno se debe sentir/NCB un verdadero boludo
one oneself must feel a real idiot
'One must feel like a real idiot'

We hypothesize that NA and NCB are specifically helped by the Spanish morphology as captured in the POS tags. This hypothesis is also supported when we consider the error reduction achieved by adding POS to the word feature only. For Chinese, the error reduction is 5.5% for CB and 4.7% for NA (derived from Tables 3 and 4), while for Spanish the error reduction is 12.1% for CB and 17.2% for NA (derived from Tables 6 and 7), suggesting that Spanish profits more from POS tags than Chinese, and crucially, Spanish NA profits more than Spanish CB.

When we compare these results to the English results reported by Prabhakaran et al. (2010), we see that without syntactic features (which we do not use in this paper), their numerical results are somewhat similar to ours. While their training set is much smaller (around 10,000 words, only a sixth of our training corpora), the results using only lexical features and POS tags are similar to ours (57% F-measure weighted average). However, when features derived from a parse tree are derived, the score goes up by 7% absolute. This is because NCB, ROB, and NA labels often correspond to syntactic configurations involving bi-clausal structures, and require an exact analysis of the lexicon-syntactic structure. This is true not only of English, but also of Chinese and Spanish. We intend to incorporate parsing in future work.

## 8 Future Work

We have seen that we can predict Committed Belief in Chinese and Spanish with acceptable accuracy for the common labels of CB and NA. Future work will concentrate on using a parser, which we expect to boost performance considerably.

## Acknowledgments

We would like to thank the four anonymous reviewers for their thoughtful and useful comments; unfortunately, we have not been able to respond to all of the comments in this version of the paper.

Rambow's work on this paper was supported by the DARPA DEFT Program. The views expressed are those of the authors and do not reflect the official policy or position of the Department of Defense or the U.S. Government.

## References

Rami Al-Rfou, Bryan Perozzi, and Steven Skiena. 2013. Polyglot: Distributed word representations for multilingual nlp. In *Proceedings of the Seventeenth Conference on Computational Natural Language Learning*, pages 183–192, Sofia, Bulgaria, August. Association for Computational Linguistics.

Mona Diab, Lori Levin, Teruko Mitamura, Owen Rambow, Vinodkumar Prabhakaran, and Weiwei Guo. 2009. Committed belief annotation and tagging. In *Proceedings of the Third Linguistic Annotation Workshop*, pages 68–73, Suntec, Singapore, August. Association for Computational Linguistics.

Christopher D. Manning, Mihai Surdeanu, John Bauer, Jenny Finkel, Steven J. Bethard, and David McClosky. 2014. The Stanford CoreNLP natural language processing toolkit. In *Association for Computational Linguistics (ACL) System Demonstrations*, pages 55–60.

Lluís Padró and Evgeny Stanilovsky. 2012. Freeling 3.0: Towards wider multilinguality. In *Proceedings of the Language Resources and Evaluation Conference (LREC 2012)*, Istanbul, Turkey, May. ELRA.

F. Pedregosa, G. Varoquaux, A. Gramfort, V. Michel, B. Thirion, O. Grisel, M. Blondel, P. Prettenhofer, R. Weiss, V. Dubourg, J. Vanderplas, A. Passos, D. Cournapeau, M. Brucher, M. Perrot, and E. Duchesnay. 2011. Scikit-learn: Machine learning in Python. *Journal of Machine Learning Research*, 12:2825–2830.

Vinodkumar Prabhakaran, Owen Rambow, and Mona Diab. 2010. Automatic committed belief tagging. In *Coling 2010: Posters*, pages 1014–1022, Beijing, China, August. Coling 2010 Organizing Committee.

Vinodkumar Prabhakaran, Tomas By, Julia Hirschberg, Owen Rambow, Samira Shaikh, Tomek Strzalkowski, Jennifer Tracey, Michael Arrigo, Rupayan Basu, Micah Clark, Adam Dalton, Mona Diab, Louise Guthrie, Anna Prokofieva, Stephanie Strassel, Gregory Werner, Yorick Wilks, and Janyce Wiebe. 2015. A new dataset and evaluation for belief/factuality. In *Proceedings of the Fourth Joint Conference on Lexical and Computational Semantics*, pages 82–91, Denver, Colorado, June. Association for Computational Linguistics.

Roser Saurí and James Pustejovsky. 2009. FactBank: a corpus annotated with event factuality. *Language Resources and Evaluation*, 43:227–268. 10.1007/s10579-009-9089-9.

Gregory Werner, Vinodkumar Prabhakaran, Mona Diab, and Owen Rambow. 2015. Committed belief tagging on the factbank and lu corpora: A comparative study. In *Proceedings of the Second Workshop on Extra-Propositional Aspects of Meaning in Computational Semantics (ExProM 2015)*, pages 32–40, Denver, Colorado, June. Association for Computational Linguistics.

# Contradiction Detection for Rumorous Claims

**Piroska Lendvai**
Computational Linguistics
Saarland University
Saarbrücken, Germany
piroska.r@gmail.com

**Uwe D. Reichel**
Research Institute for Linguistics
Hungarian Academy of Sciences
Budapest, Hungary
uwe.reichel@nytud.mta.hu

## Abstract

The utilization of social media material in journalistic workflows is increasing, demanding automated methods for the identification of mis- and disinformation. Since textual contradiction across social media posts can be a signal of rumorousness, we seek to model how claims in Twitter posts are being textually contradicted. We identify two different contexts in which contradiction emerges: its broader form can be observed across independently posted tweets and its more specific form in threaded conversations. We define how the two scenarios differ in terms of central elements of argumentation: claims and conversation structure. We design and evaluate models for the two scenarios uniformly as 3-way Recognizing Textual Entailment tasks in order to represent claims and conversation structure implicitly in a generic inference model, while previous studies used explicit or no representation of these properties. To address noisy text, our classifiers use simple similarity features derived from the string and part-of-speech level. Corpus statistics reveal distribution differences for these features in contradictory as opposed to non-contradictory tweet relations, and the classifiers yield state of the art performance.

## 1 Introduction and Task Definition

Assigning a veracity judgment to a claim appearing on social media requires complex procedures including reasoning on claims aggregated from multiple microposts, to establish claim veracity status (resolved or not) and veracity value (true or false). Until resolution, a claim circulating on social media platforms is regarded as a rumor (Mendoza et al., 2010). The detection of contradicting and disagreeing microposts supplies important cues to claim veracity processing procedures. These tasks are challenging to automatize not only due to the surface noisiness and conciseness of user generated content. One complicating factor is that claim denial or rejection is linguistically often not explicitly expressed, but appears without classical rejection markers or modality and speculation cues (Morante and Sporleder, 2012). Explicit and implicit contradictions furthermore arise in different contexts: in threaded discussions, but also across independently posted messages; both contexts are exemplified in Figure 1 on Twitter data.

Language technology has not yet solved the processing of contradiction-powering phenomena, such as negation (Morante and Blanco, 2012) and stance detection (Mohammad et al., 2016), where stance is defined to express speaker favorability towards an evaluation target, usually an entity or concept. In the veracity computation scenario we can speak of *claim targets* that are above the entity level: targets are entire rumors, such as '11 people died during the Charlie Hebdo attack'. Contradiction and stance detection have so far only marginally been addressed in the veracity context (de Marneffe et al., 2012; Ferreira and Vlachos, 2016; Lukasik et al., 2016).

We propose investigating the advantages of incorporating claim target and conversation context as premises in the Recognizing Textual Entailment (RTE) framework for contradiction detection in rumorous tweets. Our goals are manifold: (a) to offer richer context in contradiction modeling than what would be available on the level of individual tweets, the typical unit of analysis in previous studies; (b) to train and test supervised classifiers for contradiction detection in the RTE inference framework; (c) to address contradiction detection at the level of text similarity only, as opposed to semantic similarity (Xu et al., 2015); (d) to distinguish and focus on two different contradiction relationship types, each involving specific combinations of claim target mention, polarity, and contextual proximity, in particular:



*Proceedings of the Workshop on Extra-Propositional Aspects of Meaning in Computational Linguistics,*
pages 31–40, Osaka, Japan, December 12 2016.

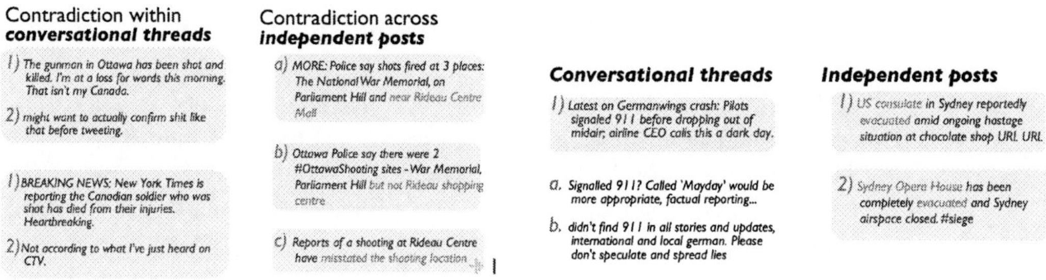


Figure 1: Explicit (far left: in threads, left: in independent posts) vs implicit (right: in threads, far right: in independent posts) contradictions in threaded discussions and in independent posts.

1. **Independent contradictions**: Contradictory relation between independent posts, in which two tweets contain different information about the same claim target that cannot simultaneously hold. The two messages are independently posted, i.e., not occurring within a structured conversation.
2. **Disagreeing replies**: Contradictory relation between a claim-originating tweet and a direct reply to it, whereby the reply expresses disagreement with respect to the claim-introducing tweet.

Contradiction between independently posted tweets typically arises in a broad discourse setting, and may feature larger distance in terms of time, space, and source of information. The claim target is mentioned in both posts in the contradiction pair, since these posts are uninformed about each other or assume uninformedness of the reader, and thus do not or can not make coreference to their shared claim target. Due to the same reason, the polarity of both posts with respect to the claim can be identical. Texts paired in this type of contradiction resemble those of the recent Interpretable Semantic Similarity shared task (Agirre et al., 2016) that calls to identify five chunk level semantic relation types (equivalence, opposition, specificity, similarity or relatedness) between two texts that originate from headlines or captions.

Disagreeing replies are more specific instances of contradiction: contextual proximity is small and trivially identifiable by means of e.g. social media platform metadata, for example the property encoding the tweet ID to which the reply was sent, which in our setup is always a thread-initiating tweet. The claim target is by definition assumed to be contained in the thread-initiating tweet (sometimes termed as claim- or rumor-source tweet). It can be the case that the claim target is not contained in the reply, which can be explained by the proximity and thus shared context of the two posts. The polarity values in source and reply must by definition be different; we refer to this scenario as Disagreeing replies. Importantly, replies may not contain a (counter-)claim on their own but some other form to express disagreement and polarity – for example in terms of speculative language use, or the presence of extra-linguistic cues such as a URL pointing to an online article that holds contradictory content. Such cues are difficult to decode for a machine, and their representation for training automatic classifiers is largely unexplored. Note that we do not make assumptions or restrictions about how the claim target is encoded textually in any of the two scenarios.

In this study, we tackle both contradiction types using a single generic approach: we recast them as three-way RTE tasks on pairs of tweets. The findings of our previous study in which semantic inference systems with sophisticated, corpus-based or manually created syntactico-semantic features were applied to contradiction-labeled data indicate the lack of robust syntactic and semantic analysis for short and noisy texts; cf. Chapter 3 in (Lendvai et al., 2016b). This motivates our current simple text similarity metrics in search of alternative methods for the contradiction processing task.

In Section 2 we introduce related work and resources, in Sections 3 and 4 present and motivate the collections and the features used for modeling. After the description of method and scores in Section 5, findings are discussed in Section 6.

## 2 Related work and resources

**Recognizing Textual Entailment (RTE)** Processing semantic inference phenomena such as contradiction, entailment and stance between text pairs has been gaining momentum in language technology. Inference has been suggested to be conveniently formalized in the generic framework of RTE[1] (Dagan et al., 2006). As an improvement over the binary Entailment vs Non-entailment scenario, three-way RTE has appeared but is still scarcely investigated (Ferreira and Vlachos, 2016; Lendvai et al., 2016a). The *Entailment* relation between two text snippets holds if the claim present in snippet B can be concluded from snippet A. The *Contradiction* relation applies when the claim in A and the claim in B cannot be simultaneously true. The *Unknown* relation applies if A and B neither entail nor contradict each other.

The RTE-3 benchmark dataset is the first resource that labels paired text snippets in terms of 3-way RTE judgments (De Marneffe et al., 2008), but it is comprised of general newswire texts. Similarly, the new large annotated corpus used for deep models for entailment (Bowman et al., 2015) labeled text pairs as Contradiction are too broadly defined, i.e., expressing generic semantic incoherence rather than semantically motivated polarization and mismatch that we are after, which questions its utility in the rumor verification context.

As far as contradiction processing is concerned, accounting for negation in RTE is the focus of a recent study (Madhumita, 2016), but it is still set according to the binary RTE setup. A standalone contradiction detection system was implemented by (De Marneffe et al., 2008), using complex rule-based features. A specific RTE application, the Excitement Open Platform[2] (Padó et al., 2015) has been developed to provide a generic platform for applied RTE. It integrates several entailment decision algorithms, while only the Maximum Entropy-based model (Wang and Neumann, 2007) is available for 3-way RTE classification. This model implements state-of-the-art linguistic preprocessing augmented with lexical resources (WordNet, VerbOcean), and uses the output of part-of-speech and dependency parsing in its structure-oriented, overlap-based approach for classification and was tested for both our tasks as explained in (Lendvai et al., 2016b).

**Stance detection** Stance classification and stance-labeled corpora are relevant for contradiction detection, because the relationship of two texts expressing opposite stance (positive and negative) can in some contexts be judged to be contradictory: this is exactly what our Disagreeing reply scenario covers. Stance classification for rumors was introduced by (Qazvinian et al., 2011) where the goal was to generate a binary (for or against) stance judgment. Stance is typically classified on the level of individual tweets: reported approaches predominantly utilize statistical models, involving supervised machine learning (de Marneffe et al., 2012) and RTE (Ferreira and Vlachos, 2016). Another relevant aspect of stance detection for our current study is the presence of the stance target in the text to be stance-labeled. A recent shared task on social media data defined separate challenges depending on whether target-specific training data is included in the task or not (Mohammad et al., 2016); the latter requires additional effort to encode information about the stance target, cf. e.g. (Augenstein et al., 2016). The PHEME project released a new stance-labeled social media dataset (Zubiaga et al., 2015) that we also utilize as described next.

## 3 Data

The two datasets corresponding to our two tasks are drawn from a freely available, annotated social media corpus[3] that was collected from the Twitter platform[4] via filtering on event-related keywords and hashtags in the Twitter Streaming API. We worked with English tweets related to four events: the Ottawa shooting[5], the Sydney Siege[6], the Germanwings crash[7], and the Charlie Hebdo shooting[8]. Each event in

[1]http://www.aclweb.org/aclwiki/index.php?title=Recognizing_Textual_Entailment

[2]http://hltfbk.github.io/Excitement-Open-Platform

[3]https://figshare.com/articles/PHEME_rumour_scheme_dataset_journalism_use_ case/2068650

[4]twitter.com

[5]https://en.wikipedia.org/wiki/2014_shootings_at_Parliament_Hill,_Ottawa

[6]https://en.wikipedia.org/wiki/2014_Sydney_hostage_crisis

[7]https://en.wikipedia.org/wiki/Germanwings_Flight_9525

[8]https://en.wikipedia.org/wiki/Charlie_Hebdo_shooting

| event | ENT | CON | UNK | #uniq clms | #uniq tws | ENT | CON | UNK | #uniq clms | #uniq tws |
|---|---|---|---|---|---|---|---|---|---|---|
| chebdo | 143 | 34 | 486 | 36 | 736 | 647 | 427 | 866 | 27 | 199 |
| gwings | 39 | 6 | 107 | 13 | 176 | 461 | 257 | 447 | 4 | 29 |
| ottawa | 79 | 37 | 292 | 28 | 465 | 555 | 377 | 168 | 18 | 125 |
| ssiege | 112 | 59 | 456 | 37 | 697 | 332 | 317 | 565 | 21 | 143 |
| | 373 | 136 | 1341 | 114 | 2074 | 1995 | 1378 | 2046 | 70 | 496 |

Table 1: *Threads* (left) and *iPosts* (right) RTE datasets compiled from 4 crisis events: amount of pairs per entailment type (*ENT, CON, UNK*), amount of unique rumorous claims (*#uniq clms*) used for creating the pairs, amount of unique tweets discussing these claims (*#uniq tws*).

the corpus was pre-annotated as explained in (Zubiaga et al., 2015) for several rumorous claims[9] – officially not yet confirmed statements lexicalized by a concise proposition, e.g. "Four cartoonists were killed in the Charlie Hebdo attack" and "French media outlets to be placed under police protection". The corpus collection method was based on a retweet threshold, therefore most tweets originate from authoritative sources using relatively well-formed language, whereas replying tweets often feature non-standard language use.

Tweets are organized into threaded conversations in the corpus and are marked up with respect to stance, certainty, evidentiality, and other veracity-related properties; for full details on released data we refer to (Zubiaga et al., 2015). The dataset on which we run disagreeing reply detection (henceforth: *Threads*) was converted by us to RTE format based on the threaded conversations labeled in this corpus. We created the Threads RTE dataset drawing on manually pre-assigned Response Type labels by (Zubiaga et al., 2015) that were meant to characterize source tweet – replying tweet relations in terms of four categories. We mapped these four categories onto three RTE labels: a reply pre-labeled as *Agreed* with respect to its source tweet was mapped to *Entailment*, a reply pre-labeled as *Disagreed* was mapped to *Contradiction*, while replies pre-labeled as *AppealforMoreInfo* and *Comment* were mapped to *Unknown*. Only direct replies to source tweets relating to the same four events as in the independent posts RTE dataset were kept. There are 1,850 tweet pairs in this set; the proportion of contradiction instances amounts to 7%. The *Threads* dataset holds *CON, ENT* and *UNK* pairs as exemplified below. Conform the RTE format, pair elements are termed *text* and *hypothesis* – note that directionality between *t* and *h* is assumed as symmetric in our current context so *t* and *h* are assigned based on token-level length.

- **CON** <t>We understand there are two gunmen and up to a dozen hostages inside the cafe under siege at Sydney.. ISIS flags remain on display 7News</t> <h>not ISIS flags</h>
- **ENT** <t>Report: Co-Pilot Locked Out Of Cockpit Before Fatal Plane Crash URL Germanwings URL</t> <h>This sounds like pilot suicide.</h>
- **UNK** <t>BREAKING NEWS: At least 3 shots fired at Ottawa War Memorial. One soldier confirmed shot - URL URL</t> <h>All our domestic military should be armed, now.</h>.

The independently posted tweets dataset (henceforth: *iPosts*) that we used for contradiction detection between independently emerging claim-initiating tweets is described in (Lendvai et al., 2016a). This collection is holds 5.4k RTE pairs generated from about 500 English tweets using semi-automatic 3-way RTE labeling, based on semantic or numeric mismatches between the rumorous claims annotated in the data. The proportion of contradictory pairs (*CON*) amounts to 25%. The two collections are quantified in Table 1. *iPosts* dataset examples are given below.

- **CON** <t>12 people now known to have died after gunmen stormed the Paris HQ of magazine CharlieHebdo URL URL</t> <h>Awful. 11 shot dead in an assault on a Paris magazine. URL CharlieHebdo URL</h>
- **ENT** <t>SYDNEY ATTACK - Hostages at Sydney cafe - Up to 20 hostages - Up to 2 gunmen - Hostages seen holding ISIS flag DEVELOPING..</t> <h>Up to 20 held hostage in Sydney Lindt Cafe siege URL URL</h>
- **UNK** <t>BREAKING: NSW police have confirmed the siege in Sydney's CBD is now over, a police officer is reportedly among the several injured.</t> <h>Update: Airspace over Sydney has been shut down. Live coverage: URL sydneysiege</h>.

[9] *Rumor, rumorous claim* and *claim* are used interchangeably throughout the paper to refer to the same concept.

## 4 Text similarity features

Data preprocessing on both datasets included screen name and hashtag sign removal and URL masking. Then, for each tweet pair we extracted vocabulary overlap and local text alignment features. The tweets were part-of-speech-tagged using the Balloon toolkit (Reichel, 2012) (PENN tagset, (Marcus et al., 1999)), normalized to lowercase and stemmed using an adapted version of the Porter stemmer (Porter, 1980). Content words were defined to belong to the set of nouns, verbs, adjectives, adverbs, and numbers, and were identified by their part of speech labels. All punctuation was removed.

### 4.1 Vocabulary overlap

Vocabulary overlap was calculated for content word stem types in terms of the Cosine similarity and the F1 score. The Cosine similarity of two tweets is defined as $C(X,Y) = \frac{|X \cap Y|}{\sqrt{|X| \cdot |Y|}}$, where $X$ and $Y$ denote the sets of content word stems in the tweet pair.

The F1 score is defined as the harmonic mean of precision and recall. Precision and recall here refer to covering the vocabulary $X$ of one tweet by the vocabulary $Y$ of another tweet (or vice versa). It is given by $F1 = 2 \cdot \frac{\frac{|X \cap Y|}{|X|} \cdot \frac{|X \cap Y|}{|Y|}}{\frac{|X \cap Y|}{|X|} + \frac{|X \cap Y|}{|Y|}}$. Again the vocabularies $X$ and $Y$ consist of stemmed content words. Just like the Cosine index, the F1 score is a symmetric similarity metric.

These two metrics are additionally applied to the content word POS label inventories within the tweet pair, which gives the four features *cosine, cosine_pos, f_score*, and *f_score_pos*, respectively.

### 4.2 Local alignment

The amount of stemmed word token overlap was measured by applying local alignment of the token sequences using the Smith-Waterman algorithm (Smith and Waterman, 1981). We chose a score function rewarding zero substitutions by $+1$, and punishing insertions, deletions, and substitutions each by 0-reset. Having filled in the score matrix $H$, alignment was iteratively applied the following way:

**while** $\max(H) \geq t$
- trace back from the cell containing this maximum the path leading to it until a zero-cell is reached
- add the substring collected on this way to the set of aligned substrings
- set all traversed cells to 0.

The threshold $t$ defines the required minimum length of aligned substrings. It is set to 1 in this study, thus it supports a complete alignment of any pair of permutations of $x$. The traversed cells are set to 0 after each iteration step to prevent that one substring would be related to more than one alignment pair. This approach would allow for two restrictions: to prevent cross alignment not just the traversed cells $[i, j]$ but for each of these cells its entire row $i$ and column $j$ needs to be set to 0. Second, if only the longest common substring is of interest, then the iteration is trivially to be stopped after the first step. Since we did not make use of these restrictions, in our case the alignment supports cross-dependencies and can be regarded as an iterative application of a longest common substring match.

From the substring pairs in tweets $x$ and $y$ aligned this way, we extracted two text similarity measures:

- *laProp*: the proportion of locally aligned tokens over both tweets $\frac{m(x)+m(y)}{n(x)+n(y)}$
- *laPropS*: the proportion of aligned tokens in the shorter tweet $\frac{m(\hat{z})}{n(\hat{z})}$, $\hat{z} = \arg\min_{z \in \{x,y\}}[n(z)]$,

where $n(z)$ denotes the number of all tokens and $m(z)$ the number of aligned tokens in tweet $z$.

### 4.3 Corpus statistics

Figures 2 and 3 show the distribution of the features introduced above each for a selected event in both datasets. Each figure half represents a dataset; each subplot shows the distribution of a feature in dependence of the three RTE classes for the selected event in that dataset.

The plots indicate a general trend over all events and datasets: the similarity features reach highest values for the ENT class, followed by CON and UNK. Kruskal-Wallis tests applied separately for all combinations of features, events and datasets confirmed these trends, revealing significant differences for all boxplot triplets ($p < 0.001$ after correction for type 1 errors in this high amount of comparisons using the false discovery rate method of (Benjamini and Yekutieli, 2001)). Dunnett post hoc tests however clarified that for 16 out of 72 comparisons (all POS similarity measures) only UNK but not ENT and CON differ significantly ($\alpha = 0.05$). Both datasets contain the same amount of non-significant cases. Nevertheless, these trends are encouraging to test whether an RTE task can be addressed by string and POS-level similarity features alone, without syntactic or semantic level tweet comparison.

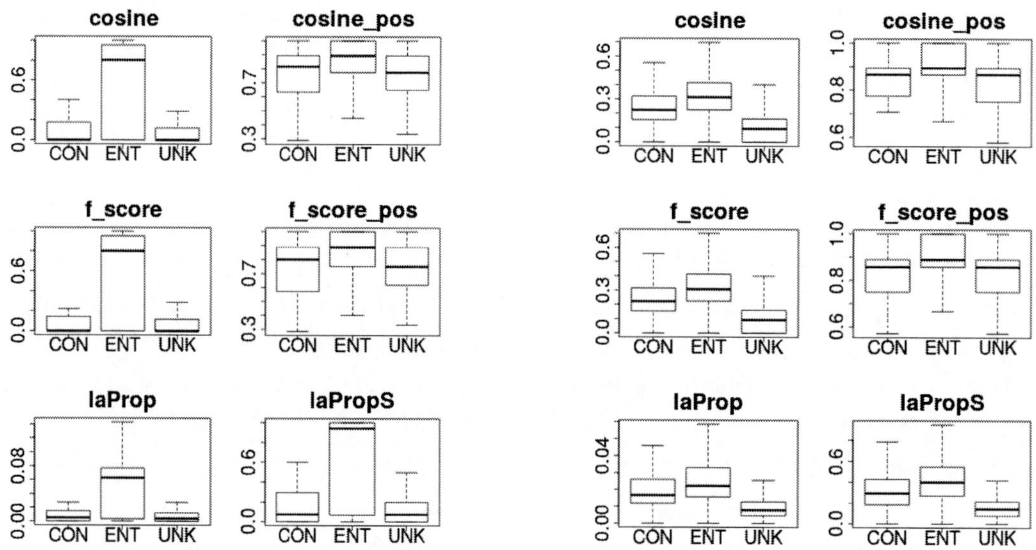


Figure 2: Distributions of the similarity metrics by tweet pair class for the event *chebdo* in the *Threads* (**left**) and the *iPosts* dataset (**right**).

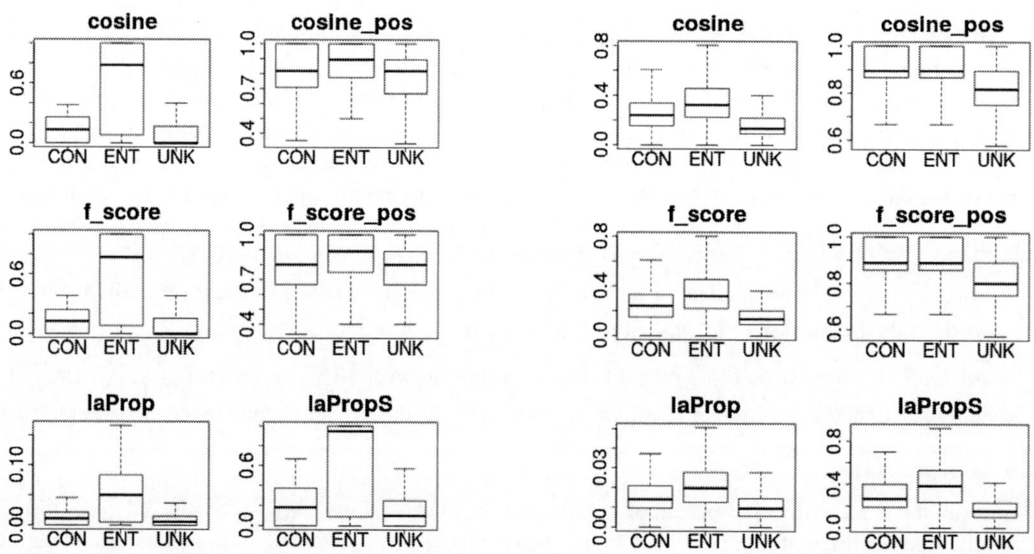


Figure 3: Distributions of the similarity metrics by tweet pair class for the event *ssiege* in the *Threads* (**left**) and the *iPosts* dataset (**right**).

## 5 RTE classification experiments for Contradiction and Disagreeing Reply detection

In order to predict the RTE classes based on the features introduced above, we trained two classifiers: Nearest (shrunken) centroids (NC) (Tibshirani et al., 2003) and Random forest (RF) (Breiman, 2001; Liaw and Wiener, 2002), using the R wrapper package *Caret* (Kuhn, 2016) with the methods *pam* and *rf*, respectively. To derive the same number of instances for all classes, we applied separately for both datasets resampling without replacement, so that the total data amounts about 4,550 feature vectors equally distributed over the three classes, the majority of 4,130 belonging to the iPosts data set. Further, we centered and scaled the feature matrix. Within the Caret framework we optimized the tunable parameters of both classifiers by maximizing the F1 score. This way the NC shrinkage delta was set to 0, which means that the class reference centroids are not modified. For RF the number of variables randomly sampled as candidates at each split was set to 2. The remaining parameters were kept default.

The classifiers were tested on both datasets in a 4-fold event-based held-out setting, training on three events and testing on the remaining one (4-fold cross-validation, CV), quantifying how performance generalizes to new events with unseen claims and unseen targets. The CV scores are summarized in Tables 2 and 3. It turns out generally that classifying CON is more difficult than classifying ENT or UNK. We observe a dependency of the classifier performances on the two contradiction scenarios: for detecting CON, RF achieved higher classification values on Threads, whereas NC performed better on iPosts. General performance across all three classes was better in independent posts than in conversational threads.

Definitions of contradiction, the genre of texts and the features used are dependent on end applications, making performance comparison nontrivial (Lendvai et al., 2016b). On a different subset of the Threads data in terms of events, size of evidence, 4 stance classes and no resampling, (Lukasik et al., 2016) report .40 overall F-score using Gaussian processes, cosine similarity on text vector representation and temporal metadata. Our previous experiments were done using the Excitement Open Platform incorporating syntactico-semantic processing and 4-fold CV. For the non-resampled Threads data we reported .11 F1 on CON via training on iPosts (Lendvai et al., 2016b). On the non-resampled iPosts data we obtained .51 overall F1 score (Lendvai et al., 2016a), F1 on CON being .25 (Lendvai et al., 2016b).

| | CON | ENT | UNK |
|---|---|---|---|
| F1 (RF/**NC**) | 0.33/**0.35** | 0.55/0.59 | 0.51/0.57 |
| precision | 0.35/0.40 | 0.54/0.61 | 0.54/0.57 |
| recall | 0.32/0.34 | 0.58/0.59 | 0.56/0.67 |
| accuracy | | 0.47/0.51 | |
| wgt F1 | | 0.48/**0.51** | |
| wgt prec. | | 0.51/0.55 | |
| wgt rec. | | 0.47/0.51 | |

Table 2: *iPosts* dataset. Mean and weighted (wgt) mean results on held-out data after event held-out cross validation for the Random Forest (RF) and Nearest Centroid (NC) classifiers.

| | CON | ENT | UNK |
|---|---|---|---|
| F1 (**RF**/NC) | **0.37**/0.11 | 0.45/0.50 | 0.40/0.36 |
| precision | 0.42/0.07 | 0.52/0.56 | 0.34/0.31 |
| recall | 0.35/0.20 | 0.41/0.47 | 0.50/0.61 |
| accuracy | | 0.42/0.39 | |
| wgt F1 | | **0.43**/0.32 | |
| wgt prec. | | 0.47/0.33 | |
| wgt rec. | | 0.42/0.39 | |

Table 3: *Threads* dataset. Mean and weighted (wgt) mean results on held-out data after event held-out cross validation for the Random forest and Nearest Centroid classifiers (RF/NC).

We proposed to model two types of contradictions: in the first both tweets encode the claim target (iPosts), in the second typically only one of them (Threads). The Nearest Centroid algorithm performs poorly on the CON class in Threads where textual overlap is typically small especially for the CON and UNK classes, in part due to the absence of the claim target in replies. However, the Random Forest algorithm's performance is not affected by this factor. The advantage of RF on the Threads data can be explained by its property of training several weak classifiers on parts of the feature vectors only. By this boosting strategy a usually undesirable combination of relatively long feature vectors but few training observations can be tackled, holding for the Threads data that due to its extreme skewedness (cf. Table 1) shrunk down to only 420 datapoints after our class balancing technique of resampling without replacement. Results indicate the benefit of RF classifiers in such sparse data cases.

The good performance of NC on the much larger amount of data in iPosts is in line with the corpus statistics reported in section 4.3, implying a reasonably small amount of class overlap. The classes are thus relatively well represented by their centroids, which is exploited by the NC classifier. However, as illustrated in Figures 2 and 3, the majority of feature distributions are generally better separated for ENT and UNK, while CON in its mid position shows more overlap to both other classes and is thus overall a less distinct category.

## 6 Conclusions and Future Work

The detection of contradiction and disagreement in microposts supplies important cues to factuality and veracity assessment, and is a central task in computational journalism. We developed classifiers in a uniform, general inference framework that differentiates two tasks based on contextual proximity of the two posts to be assessed, and if the claim target may or may not be omitted in their content. We utilized simple text similarity metrics that proved to be a good basis for contradiction classification.

Text similarity was measured in terms of vocabulary and token sequence overlap. To derive the latter, local alignment turned out to be a valuable tool: as opposed to standard global alignment (Wagner and Fischer, 1974), it can account for crossing dependencies and thus for varying sequential order of information structure in entailing text pairs, e.g. in "the cat chased the mouse" and "the mouse was chased by the cat", which are differently structured into topic and comment (Halliday, 1967). We expect contradictory content to exhibit similar trends in variation with respect to content unit order – especially in the Threads scenario, where entailment inferred from a reply can become the topic of a subsequent replying tweet. Since local alignment can resolve such word order differences, it is able to preserve text similarity of entailing tweet pairs, which is reflected in the relative *laProp* boxplot heights in Figures 2 and 3.

We have run leave-one-event-out evaluation separately on the independent posts data and on the conversational threads data, which allowed us to compare performances on collections originating from the same genre and platform, but on content where claim targets in the test data are different from the targets in the training data. Our obtained generalization performance over unseen events turns out to be in line with previous reports. Via downsampling, we achieved a balanced performance on both tasks across the three RTE classes; however, in line with previous work, even in this setup the overall performance on contradiction is the lowest, whereas detecting the lack of contradiction can be achieved with much better performance in both contradiction scenarios.

Possible extensions to our approach include incorporating more informed text similarity metrics (Bär et al., 2012), formatting phenomena (Tolosi et al., 2016), and distributed contextual representations (Le and Mikolov, 2014), the utilization of knowledge-intensive resources (Padó et al., 2015), representation of alignment on various content levels (Noh et al., 2015), and formalization of contradiction scenarios in terms of additional layers of perspective (van Son et al., 2016).

## 7 Acknowledgments

P. Lendvai was supported by the PHEME FP7 project (grant nr. 611233), U. D. Reichel by an Alexander von Humboldt Society grant. We thank anonymous reviewers for their input.

## References


Eneko Agirre, Aitor Gonzalez-Agirre, Inigo Lopez-Gazpio, Montse Maritxalar, German Rigau, and Larraitz Uria. 2016. Semeval-2016 task 2: Interpretable semantic textual similarity. *Proceedings of SemEval*, pages 512–524.

Isabelle Augenstein, Andreas Vlachos, and Kalina Bontcheva. 2016. USFD: Any-Target Stance Detection on Twitter with Autoencoders. In Saif M. Mohammad, Svetlana Kiritchenko, Parinaz Sobhani, Xiaodan Zhu, and Colin Cherry, editors, *Proceedings of the International Workshop on Semantic Evaluation*, SemEval '16, San Diego, California.

Daniel Bär, Chris Biemann, Iryna Gurevych, and Torsten Zesch. 2012. UKP: Computing semantic textual similarity by combining multiple content similarity measures. In *Proceedings of the First Joint Conference on Lexical and Computational Semantics-Volume 1: Proceedings of the main conference and the shared task, and Volume 2: Proceedings of the Sixth International Workshop on Semantic Evaluation*, pages 435–440. Association for Computational Linguistics.

Yoav Benjamini and Daniel Yekutieli. 2001. The control of the false discovery rate in multiple testing under dependency. *Annals of Statistics*, 29:1165–1188.

Samuel R. Bowman, Gabor Angeli, Christopher Potts, and Christopher D. Manning. 2015. A large annotated corpus for learning natural language inference. In *Proceedings of the 2015 Conference on Empirical Methods in Natural Language Processing*, pages 632–642, Lisbon, Portugal, September. Association for Computational Linguistics.

Leo Breiman. 2001. Random forests. *Machine Learning*, 45(1):5–32.

Ido Dagan, Oren Glickman, and Bernardo Magnini. 2006. The PASCAL recognising textual entailment challenge. In *Machine learning challenges. evaluating predictive uncertainty, visual object classification, and recognising tectual entailment*, pages 177–190. Springer.

Marie-Catherine De Marneffe, Anna N Rafferty, and Christopher D Manning. 2008. Finding contradictions in text. In *Proc. of ACL*, volume 8, pages 1039–1047.

Marie-Catherine de Marneffe, Christopher D Manning, and Christopher Potts. 2012. Did it happen? the pragmatic complexity of veridicality assessment. *Computational Linguistics*, 38(2):301–333.

William Ferreira and Andreas Vlachos. 2016. Emergent: a novel data-set for stance classification. In *Proceedings of NAACL*.

Michael Alexander Kirkwood Halliday. 1967. Notes on transitivity and theme in English, part II. *Journal of Linguistics*, 3(2):199–244.

Max Kuhn, 2016. *caret: Classification and Regression Training*. R package version 6.0-71.

Quoc V Le and Tomas Mikolov. 2014. Distributed representations of sentences and documents. In *ICML*, volume 14, pages 1188–1196.

Piroska Lendvai, Isabelle Augenstein, Kalina Bontcheva, and Thierry Declerck. 2016a. Monolingual social media datasets for detecting contradiction and entailment. In *Proc. of LREC-2016*.

Piroska Lendvai, Isabelle Augenstein, Dominic Rout, Kalina Bontcheva, and Thierry Declerck. 2016b. Algorithms for Detecting Disputed Information. Deliverable D4.2.2 for FP7-ICT Collaborative Project ICT-2013-611233 PHEME. `https://www.pheme.eu/wp-content/uploads/2016/06/D422_final.pdf`.

Andy Liaw and Matthew Wiener. 2002. Classification and regression by randomForest. *R News*, 2(3):18–22.

Michal Lukasik, P.K. Srijith, Duy Vu, Kalina Bontcheva, Arkaitz Zubiaga, and Trevor Cohn. 2016. Hawkes Processes for Continuous Time Sequence Classification: An Application to Rumour Stance Classification in Twitter. In *Proceedings of ACL-16*.

Madhumita. 2016. Recognizing textual entailment. Master's thesis, Saarland University, Saarbrücken, Germany.

Mitchell P. Marcus, Ann Taylor, Robert MacIntyre, Ann Bies, Constance Cooper, Mark Ferguson, and Alison Littman. 1999. The Penn Treebank Project. `http://www.cis.upenn.edu/~treebank/home.html`. visited on Sep 29th 2016.

Marcelo Mendoza, Barbara Poblete, and Carlos Castillo. 2010. Twitter Under Crisis: Can We Trust What We RT? In *Proceedings of the First Workshop on Social Media Analytics (SOMA'2010)*, pages 71–79, New York, NY, USA. ACM.

Saif M. Mohammad, Svetlana Kiritchenko, Parinaz Sobhani, Xiaodan Zhu, and Colin Cherry. 2016. SemEval-2016 Task 6: Detecting stance in tweets. In *Proceedings of the International Workshop on Semantic Evaluation*, SemEval '16, San Diego, California.

Roser Morante and Eduardo Blanco. 2012. *SEM 2012 shared task: Resolving the scope and focus of negation. In *Proceedings of the First Joint Conference on Lexical and Computational Semantics*.

Roser Morante and Caroline Sporleder, editors. 2012. *ExProm '12: Proceedings of the ACL-2012 Workshop on Extra-Propositional Aspects of Meaning in Computational Linguistics*. Association for Computational Linguistics.

Tae-Gil Noh, Sebastian Padó, Vered Shwartz, Ido Dagan, Vivi Nastase, Kathrin Eichler, Lili Kotlerman, and Meni Adler. 2015. Multi-level alignments as an extensible representation basis for textual entailment algorithms. *Lexical and Computational Semantics (* SEM 2015)*, page 193.

Sebastian Padó, Tae-Gil Noh, Asher Stern, Rui Wang, and Roberto Zanoli. 2015. Design and Realization of a Modular Architecture for Textual Entailment. *Natural Language Engineering*, 21(02):167–200.

Martin F. Porter. 1980. An algorithm for suffix stripping. *Program*, 14(3):130–137.

Vahed Qazvinian, Emily Rosengren, Dragomir R. Radev, and Qiaozhu Mei. 2011. Rumor has it: Identifying misinformation in microblogs. In *Proceedings of the Conference on Empirical Methods in Natural Language Processing*, EMNLP '11, pages 1589–1599.

Uwe D. Reichel. 2012. PermA and Balloon: Tools for string alignment and text processing. In *Proc. Interspeech*, page paper no. 346, Portland, Oregon, USA.

Temple F. Smith and Michael S. Waterman. 1981. Identification of common molecular subsequences. *Journal of Molecular Biology*, 147:195–197.

Robert Tibshirani, Trevor Hastie, Balasubramanian Narasimhan, and Gilbert Chu. 2003. Class prediction by nearest shrunken centroids,with applications to DNA microarrays. *Statistical Science*, 18(1):104–117.

Laura Tolosi, Andrey Tagarev, and Georgi Georgiev. 2016. An analysis of event-agnostic features for rumour classification in twitter. In *Proc. of Social Media in the Newsroom Workshop*.

Chantal van Son, Tommaso Caselli, Antske Fokkens, Isa Maks, Roser Morante, Lora Aroyo, and Piek Vossen. 2016. GRaSP: A Multilayered Annotation Scheme for Perspectives. In *Proceedings of the 10th Edition of the Language Resources and Evaluation Conference (LREC)*.

Robert A. Wagner and Michael J. Fischer. 1974. The string-to-string correction problem. *Journal of the Association for Computing Machinery*, 21(1):168–173.

Rui Wang and Günter Neumann. 2007. Recognizing textual entailment using a subsequence kernel method. In *AAAI*, volume 7, pages 937–945.

Wei Xu, Chris Callison-Burch, and William B Dolan. 2015. SemEval-2015 Task 1: Paraphrase and semantic similarity in Twitter (PIT). *Proceedings of SemEval*.

Arkaitz Zubiaga, Maria Liakata, Rob Procter, Kalina Bontcheva, and Peter Tolmie. 2015. Towards Detecting Rumours in Social Media. *CoRR*, abs/1504.04712.

# Negation and Modality in Machine Translation
# Invited talk

**Preslav Nakov**
Qatar Computing Research Institute, HBKU
pnakov@qf.org.qa

## Abstract

Negation and modality are two important grammatical phenomena that have attracted recent research attention as they can contribute to extra-propositional meaning aspects, among with factuality, attribution, irony and sarcasm. These aspects go beyond analysis such as semantic role labeling, and modeling them is important as a step towards a higher level of language understanding, which is needed for practical applications such as sentiment analysis. In this talk, I will go beyond English, and I will discuss how negation and modality are expressed in other languages. I will also go beyond sentiment analysis and I will present some challenges that the two phenomena pose for machine translation (MT). In particular, I will demonstrate how contemporary MT systems fail on them, and I will discuss some possible solutions.



*Proceedings of the Workshop on Extra-Propositional Aspects of Meaning in Computational Linguistics*, page 41, Osaka, Japan, December 12 2016.

# Problematic Cases in the Annotation of Negation in Spanish

**Salud María Jiménez-Zafra[1], M. Teresa Martín-Valdivia[1], L. Alfonso Ureña-López[1], M. Antònia Martí[2], Mariona Taulé[2]**

[1]Department of Computer Science, Universidad de Jaén,
Campus Las Lagunillas, E-23071, Jaén, Spain
{sjzafra, maite, laurena}@ujaen.es

[2] CLiC, Centre de Llenguatge i Computació, Department of Linguistics,
University of Barcelona, 08007, Barcelona, Spain
{amarti, mtaule}@ub.edu

## Abstract

This paper presents the main sources of disagreement found during the annotation of the Spanish *SFU Review Corpus* with negation (*SFU Review$_{SP}$-NEG*). Negation detection is a challenge in most of the task related to NLP, so the availability of corpora annotated with this phenomenon is essential in order to advance in tasks related to this area. A thorough analysis of the problems found during the annotation could help in the study of this phenomenon.

## 1 Introduction

Negation is a key element in tasks related to Natural Language Processing (NLP) that has generated special interest in the research community during the last years, such as Sentiment Analysis, Information Extraction and Question Answering. It is a complex linguistic phenomenon that requires a deep analysis. The availability of corpora annotated with negation is essential for carrying out a study of this phenomenon. Actually, most of the available corpora are for English language (Pyysalo et al., 2007; Kim et al., 2008; Vincze et al., 2008; Councill et al., 2010; Konstantinova et al., 2012; Morante and Daelemans, 2012; Bokharaeian et al., 2014; Blanco and Moldovan, 2014; Banjade and Rus, 2016). However, the presence of languages other than English on the Internet is greater every day and, consequently, the development of systems able to deal with negation in these other languages is a necessity. Due to this fact, we decided to annotate a Spanish corpus with negation. Moreover, taking into account the importance of negation in texts that express opinions since it directly affects their polarity, we also annotated how negation affects the polarity of the words that are within its scope.

The Spanish *SFU Review Corpus* (Taboada et al., 2006) was selected for the annotation because of its multi-domain nature and the fact that it is widely known in the domain of Sentiment Analysis and Opinion Mining. The English version of the *SFU Review Corpus* was annotated at the token level with negative and speculative keywords and at the sentence level with their linguistic scope (Konstantinova et al., 2012). The authors used the guidelines defined by Vincze (2010), but they adapted the annotation scheme to the review domain (Konstantinova and De Sousa, 2011). Although we considered these guidelines, after a thorough analysis of negation in Spanish, we defined criteria more suitable to the typology of negation patterns in this language (Martí et al., 2016).

In this work, we show the main problems found during the annotation of negation for the Spanish *SFU Review Corpus* (*SFU Review$_{SP}$-NEG*). The annotation scheme defined is briefly described in Section 2. Following, the main sources of disagreement are presented in Section 3. Finally, conclusion and future works are outlined in Section 4.

## 2 Annotation scheme

The *SFU Review$_{SP}$-NEG* corpus[1] consists of 400 reviews of cars, hotels, washing machines, books, cell phones, music, computers and movies extracted from the Ciao.es website. Each domain contains 25 positive and 25 negative reviews. We annotated each review at token level with the lemma and the



[1]http://sinai.ujaen.es/sfu-review-sp-neg-2/



*Proceedings of the Workshop on Extra-Propositional Aspects of Meaning in Computational Linguistics*, pages 42–48, Osaka, Japan, December 12 2016.

PoS and at sentence level with negation markers or negation cues, their linguistic scope and the event. We also annotated how negation affects the words that are within its scope (if there is a change in the polarity or an increment or reduction of its value), which is very useful for Sentiment Analysis. The general annotation scheme followed can be seen in Figure 1.

```
<review polarity= 'positive/negative'>
 <sentence complex='yes/no'>
  <neg_structure
   polarity='positive/negative/neutral'
   change='yes/no'
   polarity_modifier='increment/reduction'
   value='neg/contrast/comp/noneg'>
   <scope>
    <negexp discid='1n/1c'>
    </negexp>
    <event>
    </event>
   </scope>
  </neg_structure>
 </sentence>
</review>
```

Figure 1: General annotation scheme.

The labels used for the annotation of negation in the corpus are described briefly below:

- **<review polarity="positive/negative">**. The attribute **polarity** describes the polarity of the review, which can be *"positive"* or *"negative"*, according to the value assigned to it in the Spanish *SFU Review Corpus*.

- **<sentence complex="yes/no">**. The label *sentence* corresponds to a complete sentence, a phrase or a fragment/chunk of a sentence in which a negative structure can occur. In *SFU Review*$_{SP}$*-NEG*, we only annotate the structures that contain at least one negation marker or negation cue. Therefore, sentences without negation markers are not labeled. This label has the attribute **complex** assigned to it and it can take one of the following values:
  - *"yes"*, if the sentence contains more than one negative structure *<neg_structure>* (1a).

    1a. **<sentence complex="yes">** Sin embargo, **<neg_structure>** las habitaciones no están cuidadas **</neg_structure>**,hay manchas de humedad, techos desconchados, **<neg_structure>** las TV no tienen mando a distancia **</neg_structure>**, los suelos de los pasillos están levantados, necesita una remodelación urgente! **</sentence>**
    'However, the rooms are not well maintained, there are humidity stains, peeling ceilings, there is no TV remote control, the floors of the halls are raised, it needs urgent renovation!'

  - *"no"*, if the sentence contains only one negative structure (2a).

    2a. **<sentence complex="no">** **<neg_structure>** No hay en la habitación ni una triste hoja para ver qué hay para comer **</neg_structure>** **</sentence>**

'The room does not have nor a sad sheet to see what's for lunch.'

- <**neg_structure**>. This label corresponds to a syntactic structure in which a negation marker or a negation cue occurs. It has 4 attributes assigned to it, and two of which (**change** and **polarity_modifier**) are mutually exclusive (1b, 2b):
  - **polarity**: indicates the semantic orientation of the negative structure, i.e., whether it is *"positive"*, *"negative"* or *"neutral"*.
  - **change**: states whether the polarity or the meaning of the negative structure has been totally modified (change=*"yes"*) or not (change=*"no"*) because of the negation.
  - **polarity_modifier**: indicates whether the negative structure contains an element that nuances its polarity. If there is an increment in the intensity of the polarity value it takes the value *"increment"* and, in contrast, if there is a diminishing of the polarity value it takes the value *"reduction"*.
  - **value**: shows the meaning of the negative structure, that is to say, if it expresses negation (*"neg"*); if it indicates contrast or opposition between terms (*"contrast"*); if it expresses a comparison or inequality between terms (*"comp"*) or if it does not negate (*"noneg"*) despite containing a negation marker o cue.

  1b. <sentencecomplex="yes"> Sin embargo, **<neg_structure polarity="negative" change="yes" value="neg">** las habitaciones no están cuidadas **</neg_structure>**, hay manchas de humedad, techos desconchados, **<neg_structure polarity="negative" change="yes" value="neg">** las TV no tienen mando a distancia **</neg_structure>**, los suelos de los pasillos están levantados, necesita una remodelación urgente! </sentence>
  'However, the rooms are not well maintained, there are humidity stains, peeling ceilings, there is no TV remote control, the floors of the halls are raised, it needs urgent renovation!'

  2b. <sentence complex="no"> **<neg_structure polarity="negative" polarity_modifier="increment" value="neg">** No hay en la habitación ni una triste hoja para ver qué hay para comer **</neg_structure>** </sentence>
  'The room does not have nor a sad sheet to see what's for lunch.'

- <**scope**>. The label scope delimits the part of the negative structure that is within the scope of negation (1c, 2c). It includes both the negation marker or cue (<**negexp**>) and the event (<**event**>).

- <**negexp**>. This label corresponds to the word(s) that express(es) negation (1c, 2c). It can have the attribute **discid** associated to it if negation is expressed by more than one negative element and they are discontinuous (2c).

- <**event**>. The label event denotes the words that are directly affected by negation (usually verbs or adjectives) (1c, 2c). It is usually part of the scope, though it can also match the scope.

  1c. <sentencecomplex="yes"> Sin embargo, <neg_structure polarity="negative" change="yes" value="neg"> <**scope**> las habitaciones <**negexp**> no <**/negexp**> <**event**> están cuidadas <**/event**> <**/scope**> </neg_structure>, hay manchas de humedad, techos desconchados, <neg_structure polarity="negative" change="yes" value="neg"> <**scope**> las TV <**negexp**> no <**/negexp**> <**event**> tienen <**/event**> mando a distancia <**/scope**> </neg_structure>, los suelos de los pasillos están levantados, necesita una remodelación urgente! </sentence>
  'However, the rooms are not well maintained, there are humidity stains, peeling ceilings, there is no TV remote control, the floors of the halls are raised, it needs urgent renovation!'

2c. <sentence complex="no"> <neg_structure polarity="negative" polarity_modifier="increment" value="neg"> **<scope>** **<negexp discid="1n">** No **</negexp>** **<event>** hay **</event>** en la habitación **<negexp discid="1c">** ni **</negexp>** una triste hoja **</scope>** para ver qué hay para comer </neg_structure> </sentence>
'The room does not have nor a sad sheet to see what's for lunch.'

## 3 Problematic cases

Two types of annotations problems should be distinguished concerning negation: a) those that are related to the lack of agreement between the annotators, since what it is being annotated is complex: especially the scope, but also the event, and the discontinuities; and b) the problems arising from how the negation pattern is interpreted. These cases occur in constructions that are at the limit of what can be considered negation. They are semantic problems, i.e., problems involved in interpreting these constructions. In our typology, these cases mainly correspond to negation patterns in comparative and contrastive constructions.

### 3.1 Disagreement cases

The corpus was annotated by 4 annotators: two trained annotators who carried out the annotation task and two senior researchers with experience in corpus annotation who supervised the whole process. Firstly, a training phase was carried out in which 50 files were annotated in parallel by the trained annotators in order to refine the annotation guidelines. After that, a further 50 files were annotated individually by the same annotators to measure inter-annotator agreement with the aim of detecting and resolving problematic cases. A total of 528 negative structures were annotated and 49 cases of disagreement were found. An observed agreement of 90.72% corresponding to a kappa-score of 0.74 was observed in the inter-annotator agreement test. We then proceeded to annotate the whole corpus. We will now discuss the main sources of disagreement (Table 1).

| Type of disagreement | #Total | % diagreement in 528 <neg_structure> | % disagreement of 49 disagreement elements |
|---|---|---|---|
| <scope> boundary | 16 | 3.03% | 32.65% |
| <event> boundary | 15 | 2.84% | 30.61% |
| <neg_structure> extension | 10 | 1.89% | 20.40% |
| Discontinuous elements | 8 | 1.51% | 16.32% |
| **Disagreements (total)** | **49** | **9.28%** | |

Table 1: Disagreements cases.

Most of the problematic cases (63.26%) were related to the scope of the negation and the event, though disagreements related to the value of the attributes of the <neg_structure> label and to discontinuities were also observed. Below, we describe these cases with a representative example[2]:

- Disagreements related to the scope of negation: 16 disagreements were due to the non-inclusion of the relative pronoun within the scope (3). We decided to include the relative pronoun (the subject of the relative clause) in the scope, therefore in the *SFU Review$_{SP}$-NEG* corpus the subject is always included within the scope when the word directly affected by negation is the verb of the sentence (3b):

  3. (a) Una cámara de fotos **que** **<scope>** no es una maravilla **</scope>**
     (b) Una cámara de fotos **<scope>** **que** no es una maravilla **</scope>**
     'A photo camera that is not so fantastic.'

[2]For all cases, the annotation used in the second example (labeled with letter *b*) was selected. Disagreements were discussed by all the annotators and solutions were proposed by the senior researchers.

- Disagreements related to the event were mainly due to the treatment of verbal forms: pronominal verbs and light verbs. We observed a total of 15 cases. The problem with the pronominal verbs was the non-inclusion of the pronoun inside the event (4). In this case, we opted to include the pronoun inside the event (4b), since it is part of the verb:

  4. (a) <negexp> No </negexp> <**event**> he podido resistir <**/event**> **me**
     (b) <negexp> No </negexp> <**event**> he podido resistir **me** <**/event**>
     'I could not resist myself.'

  On the other hand, the problem with the light verbs arose from the incorrect identification of the lexicalized arguments. In (5) the argument *una rallada* ('a scratch') was incorrectly treated as a lexicalized form, whereas in (6) the opposite is the case: *tan mal* is part of the verbal form (the complete verbal form should be: *dejar (tan) mal*).

  5. (a) <negexp discid="1n"> No </negexp> <**event**> tenía
     <negexp discid="1c"> ni </negexp> **una rallada** <**/event**>
     (b) <negexp discid="1n"> No </negexp> <**event**> tenía <**/event**>
     <negexp discid="1c"> ni </negexp> una rallada
     'It did not have a single scratch.'

  6. (a) <negexp> No </negexp> lo <**event**> dejaré <**/event**> **tan mal**
     (b) <negexp discid="1n"> No </negexp> lo <**event**> dejaré
     <negexp discid="1c"> **tan** </negexp> **mal** <**/event**>
     'I will not leave him so badly.'

- 10 disagreements were found in the value of the attributes of the <neg_structure> label. Most of them were related to the value of the attributes *polarity* and *value*. For instance, in (7) the negation structure was annotated as if it expressed negation (value="neg"), whereas the correct value should be "contrast". In (8), the annotator forgot to assign the value of the attribute *value* to the negative structure.

  7. (a) Los motorolas a mí <**neg_structure value= "neg"**
     **polarity="negative"**> no hacen más que darme problemas <**neg_structure**>
     (b) Los motorolas a mí <**neg_structure value= "contrast"**
     **polarity="negative"**> no hacen más que darme problemas <**neg_structure**>
     'Motorolas (devices) have not given me anything but trouble.'

  8. (a) <**neg_structure value=**> no me puedo mover <**neg_structure**>
     (b) <**neg_structure value="neg"**> no me puedo mover <**neg_structure**>
     'I can not move (about).'

- Disagreements related to discontinuities were due to the non-identification of intensifiers (9) and diminishers (10). In both of the following examples, the annotator failed to identify the discontinuous negative expression, the intensifier *para nada* ('at all') and the diminisher *del todo* ('completely') were not annotated.

  9. (a) <negexp> no </negexp> me <event> extraña< /event> **para nada** los problemas que tiene
     (b) <**negexp discid="1n"**> no <**/negexp**> me <event> extraña< /event> <**negexp discid="1c"**> **para nada** <**/negexp**> los problemas que tiene
     'I am not surprised at all by the problems he is having.'

10. (a) <negexp> no </negexp> <event> estaba **del todo** acertado < /event>
    (b) **<negexp discid="1n">** no **</negexp>** <event> estaba
    **<negexp discid="1c"> del todo </negexp>** acertado < /event>
    'It was not completely right.'

### 3.2 Semantic interpretation of negation patterns

In this section we present the cases that generated the greatest controversy during the annotation process. They are borderline cases in which it is difficult to determine whether negation patterns express negation or not. These cases are related to comparative constructions (3.2.1) and contrastive constructions (3.2.2):

#### 3.2.1 Comparative constructions

In the case of comparative constructions, the negation simply places an entity below or above another entity on a scale. What is negated is the predicate expressing somebody's beliefs. In sample (11), what is negated is the predicate *imaginaba* ('imaginated'). In this type of constructions we decided that there is no negation, strictly speaking, and we annotated them with the value 'comp' for 'comparative'. Example (11) can be paraphrased as *Me lo imaginaba más grande* ('I imagined it bigger') or *Es más pequeño de lo que me imaginaba* ('It is smaller than I imagined'). In both cases no negation is present.

11. **No** es **tan** grande **como** me lo imaginaba.
    'It is **not as** big **as** I imagined.'

Many of these cases are examples of what is called 'downward entailment operators', which are controversial and closely related to negation, but are not featured in this version of the corpus.

#### 3.2.2 Contrastive constructions

Contrastive constructions are used to counterpoise different assessments, either to make a correction (12) or to add new information (13). In other cases, they can express obligation (14). We agreed to annotate these structures with the value 'contrast'.

12. **No** vinieron 2 soldados, **sino** 6.
    'Six soldiers came, **not** two.'

13. **No solo** lleva rueda de recambio **sino también** caja de herramientas.
    'It **not only** has a spare tire **but also** a toolbox.'

14. **No** hay más solución **que** comprar una lavadora.
    'There is **no** other solution **than** to buy a washing machine.'

Example (12) declares/states that six soldiers came and the negation refers to a supposed information about the number of soldiers who came. The function of the negation is to contrast the belief with what really happened.

Example (13) is a very common coordination construction: *no solo... sino también* ('not only... but also'). The sentence can be paraphrased as *Lleva rueda de recambio y caja de herramientas* ('It has spare tire and toolbox').

Finally, example (14) is another case of a pattern that is used to reinforce what is said. The sentence can be paraphrased as an affirmative one *La única solución es comprar una lavadora* ('The only solution is to buy a washing machine').

## 4 Conclusions and further work

In this work we have presented the main sources of disagreement detected during the annotation with negation of the Spanish *SFU Review Corpus*. We hope this will help in future annotations of this phenomenon. We have also briefly presented the annotation scheme that we defined for the annotation. We think that the availability of corpora annotated at this level is essential for developing systems that take into account negation; consequently, a thorough analysis of this phenomenon is needed.

Our future lines of research are related to using the corpus to develop a system to generate a model that uses the information annotated in it in order to automatically detect negation and its scope. Furthermore, we aim to create a lexicon of simple and complex negation markers. On the other hand, we also intend to demonstrate the importance of a corpus annotated with negation for Sentiment Analysis.

## Acknowledgements

This work has been partially supported by a Grant from the Ministerio de Educación, Cultura y Deporte (MECD - scholarship FPU014/00983), Fondo Europeo de Desarrollo Regional (FEDER) and REDES project (TIN2015-65136-C2-1-R) from the Ministerio de Economía y Competitividad. We would like to thank Maite Taboada and her team for sharing the useful SFU resource with the research community.

## References

Rajendra Banjade and Vasile Rus. 2016. Dt-neg: Tutorial dialogues annotated for negation scope and focus in context. In Nicoletta Calzolari (Conference Chair), Khalid Choukri, Thierry Declerck, Sara Goggi, Marko Grobelnik, Bente Maegaard, Joseph Mariani, Helene Mazo, Asuncion Moreno, Jan Odijk, and Stelios Piperidis, editors, *Proceedings of the Tenth International Conference on Language Resources and Evaluation (LREC 2016)*, Paris, France, may. European Language Resources Association (ELRA).

Eduardo Blanco and Dan Moldovan. 2014. Retrieving implicit positive meaning from negated statements. *Natural Language Engineering*, 20(04):501–535.

Behrouz Bokharaeian, Alberto Diaz, Mariana Neves, and Virginia Francisco. 2014. Exploring negation annotations in the drugddi corpus. In *Fourth Workshop on Building and Evaluating Resources for Health and Biomedical Text Processing (BIOTxtM 2014)*. Citeseer.

Isaac G Councill, Ryan McDonald, and Leonid Velikovich. 2010. What's great and what's not: learning to classify the scope of negation for improved sentiment analysis. In *Proceedings of the workshop on negation and speculation in natural language processing*, pages 51–59. Association for Computational Linguistics.

Jin-Dong Kim, Tomoko Ohta, and Jun'ichi Tsujii. 2008. Corpus annotation for mining biomedical events from literature. *BMC bioinformatics*, 9(1):1.

Natalia Konstantinova and Sheila CM De Sousa. 2011. Annotating negation and speculation: the case of the review domain. In *RANLP Student Research Workshop*, pages 139–144.

Natalia Konstantinova, Sheila CM De Sousa, Noa P Cruz Díaz, Manuel J Maña López, Maite Taboada, and Ruslan Mitkov. 2012. A review corpus annotated for negation, speculation and their scope. In *LREC*, pages 3190–3195.

M Antónia Martí, M Teresa Martín-Valdivia, Mariona Taulé, Salud María Jiménez-Zafra, Montserrat Nofre, and Laia Marsó. 2016. La negación en español: análisis y tipología de patrones de negación. *Procesamiento del Lenguaje Natural*, 57:41–48.

Roser Morante and Walter Daelemans. 2012. Conandoyle-neg: Annotation of negation in conan doyle stories. In *Proceedings of the Eighth International Conference on Language Resources and Evaluation, Istanbul*. Citeseer.

Sampo Pyysalo, Filip Ginter, Juho Heimonen, Jari Björne, Jorma Boberg, Jouni Järvinen, and Tapio Salakoski. 2007. Bioinfer: a corpus for information extraction in the biomedical domain. *BMC bioinformatics*, 8(1):1.

Maite Taboada, Caroline Anthony, and Kimberly Voll. 2006. Methods for creating semantic orientation dictionaries. In *Proceedings of the 5th Conference on Language Resources and Evaluation (LREC'06)*, pages 427–432.

Veronika Vincze, György Szarvas, Richárd Farkas, György Móra, and János Csirik. 2008. The bioscope corpus: biomedical texts annotated for uncertainty, negation and their scopes. *BMC bioinformatics*, 9(11):1.

Veronika Vincze. 2010. Speculation and negation annotation in natural language texts: what the case of bioscope might (not) reveal. In *Proceedings of the Workshop on Negation and Speculation in Natural Language Processing*, pages 28–31. Association for Computational Linguistics.

# Building a Dictionary of Affixal Negations

**Chantal van Son** **Emiel van Miltenburg** **Roser Morante**
Vrije Universiteit Amsterdam
{c.m.van.son, emiel.van.miltenburg, r.morantevallejo}@vu.nl

## Abstract

This paper discusses the need for a dictionary of affixal negations and regular antonyms to facilitate their automatic detection in text. Without such a dictionary, affixal negations are very difficult to detect. In addition, we show that the set of affixal negations is not homogeneous, and that different NLP tasks may require different subsets. A dictionary can store the subtypes of affixal negations, making it possible to select a certain subset or to make inferences on the basis of these subtypes. We take a first step towards creating an affixal negation dictionary by annotating all direct antonym pairs in WordNet using an existing typology of affixal negations. By highlighting some of the issues that were encountered in this annotation experiment, we hope to provide some insights into the necessary steps of building a negation dictionary.

## 1 Introduction

Affixal negations can be defined as words marked with a negative affix (in English, either the prefixes *un-*, *in-*, *dis-*, *a-*, *an-*, *non-*, *im-*, *il-*, *ir-*, or the suffix *-less*). As they typically flag the absence of particular features, detecting affixal negations is very useful for natural language processing tasks such as text mining, recognizing textual entailment, paraphrasing, or question answering. Despite their simple definition, affixal negations are very difficult to detect automatically without a substantial false positive rate. Blanco and Moldovan (2011) note:

> "No simple search could unequivocally distinguish between a negated word such as *ineffective* and the words that just happen to begin with the letters of a negative prefix, such as *invite*. The problem could be partially solved by checking if, after removal of the prefix, the word is still valid. This method mismarks *inform* as negation because *form* is a valid word. To complicate matters further, some words are valid both as negated base words and as words in their own right: The adjective *invalid* means *not valid*, while the noun *invalid* describes a disabled person." (Blanco and Moldovan, 2011, p. 232)

Blanco and Moldavan conclude that the field might be best served by a dictionary-based approach; once we have a list of affixal negations (ideally along with their antonyms), it becomes trivial to detect this kind of negation through a simple string-matching algorithm. Before we can produce such a list, however, we first need to agree on a set of annotation guidelines describing what constitutes an affixal negation, and what does not. This paper aims to highlight some of the main issues to be considered when building a negation dictionary, and reports on a first attempt to build one.

This paper is structured as follows. In Section 2, we explore the full range of lexical negation, explaining how regular antonyms and affixal negations are two sides of the same coin. We show that there are different semantic categories of lexical negation and argue that their relevance is determined by the task to be solved. Section 3 reports on an annotation experiment in which all antonym pairs in WordNet (Miller, 1995; Fellbaum, 1998b) were annotated with the subtypes of affixal negations defined by Joshi (2012).





*Proceedings of the Workshop on Extra-Propositional Aspects of Meaning in Computational Linguistics*, pages 49–56, Osaka, Japan, December 12 2016.

Section 4 provides a follow-up discussion on the requirements of a negation dictionary (based on what we learned from the annotation experiment) and its limits for automatic detection. Finally, we conclude our paper in Section 5.

## 2 Defining lexical negation

This section aims to define affixal negation from a broad natural language processing perspective. We first discuss the Conan Doyle negation corpus (Morante and Daelemans, 2012), which has a narrow definition of 'affixal negation'. We argue that this definition is the result of the task that Morante and Daelemans (2012) envisioned for their corpus. Following this observation, we explore the range of lexical negations. First, in Section 2.2, we argue that there's hardly any *semantic* reason to not to study antonyms along with affixal negation, since both are marked and express an opposition to something else. Then, in Section 2.3, we review some literature on semantic categorization of lexical negation, revealing that there is a rich landscape of affixal negations beyond the commonly studied subclass of direct negations.

### 2.1 Affixal negation

Affixal negation can be defined as a type of negation that is marked by the presence of a negative affix. However, not every affixal negation is relevant for each task; its relevance is determined by the semantics of the affixal negation and the goal of the task at hand. For example, Morante and Daelemans (2012) included affixal negations as part of their annotations of negation information at sentence level in two Conan Doyle stories. In the guidelines that were provided for these annotations, Morante et al. (2011) describe their main goal as follows:

> In these guidelines we aim at describing how to annotate the words that express negation and the part of a sentence that is affected by the negation words. The words that express negation are called *negation cues* and the part of the sentence that is affected by a negation cue is called the *scope*. [...] The final goal of annotating negation cues and their scope is to determine which events in the sentence are affected by the negation. (Morante et al., 2011, p. 3-4)

Morante et al. (2011) use a narrow definition of affixal negation, in which not all negative affixes are negation cues. According to the guidelines, a word with a negative affix is only considered an affixal negation if the meaning of the affixed word is a direct antonym of its non-affixed counterpart. So *unclear* is an affixal negation, because its meaning is the opposite of *clear*. This can be contrasted with examples such as *unspoken* (which does not mean 'not spoken', but 'understood without the need for words') and *disappear* (which does not mean 'not appear', but 'to pass out of sight; vanish'). Despite these words having some negative meaning component, they are not considered affixal negations.

The choice of what type of affixal negation to include in a dictionary or annotation task depends on the goal of the task to be solved. The narrow definition used by Morante et al. (2011) is a direct consequence of their main goal: to annotate information relative to the negative polarity of an event. The resulting corpus is meant to support the development of a system that can distinguish between facts and counterfacts. Therefore, they focus exclusively on negations that turn an event into a negated event, disregarding any expression that does not meet this criterion. As a consequence, affixal negations are only annotated if the affix negates the event or property expressed by its base. For other tasks, however, it may be relevant to include other kinds of affixal negations. In the context of sentiment analysis it all depends on whether or not the affixal derivative or its base is opinionated; words like *flawless* or *disqualify* should be included in a polarity lexicon (Wiegand et al., 2010), whereas words like *untie* or *backless* would be irrelevant. In the context of question answering, however, knowing what the word *backless* entails is essential to know the answer to the question *does the dress have a closed back?*

### 2.2 Regular antonyms

In the previous subsection we have argued that, depending on its goal, the task to be solved may require a certain subset of affixal negations. On the other hand, the full set of affixal negations may still not be sufficient if the task requires taking all sorts of opposites into account. That is, regular antonyms might have to be considered in addition to affixal negations. After all, the difference between the two categories is only morphological. The items in (1) illustrate our point; all entail the falsehood of their positive counterpart (*tasteful, delicious, great*):

(1) a. distasteful (a 'true' affixal negation)
b. disgusting (only etymologically an affixal negation)
c. dead (a regular antonym)

Moreover, we might consider these items as points on a *continuous scale* going from explicitly (1a) to implicitly (1c) marked lexical items.[1] Joshi (2012) uses the term *lexical negation* to denote both affixal negations and antonyms, leading to the taxonomy in Figure 1 (the difference between direct and indirect negation will be discussed in the next section). This taxonomy, we argue, shows the full picture that NLP researchers interested in negation ought to consider.

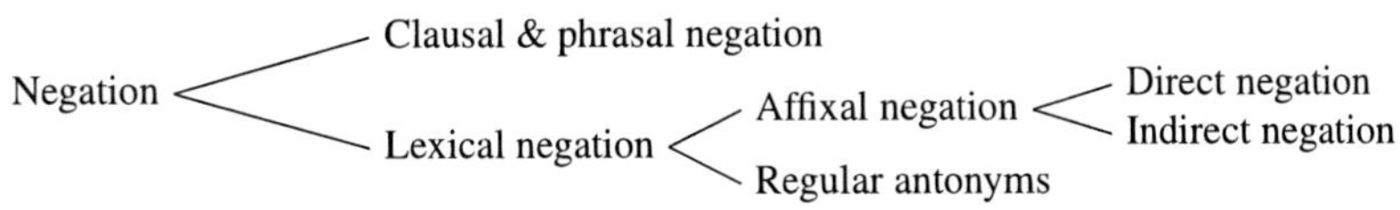


Figure 1: Taxonomy of negations, based on (Joshi, 2012).

To some extent, WordNet (Miller, 1995; Fellbaum, 1998b) and thesauri such as Roget's (Roget, 1911) already provide a collection of lexical negations. In WordNet, antonymy is defined as a lexical relation between individual lexemes that have clear opposite meanings (rather than between concepts, i.e. all the members of a synset). These 'direct antonym' pairs, such as *wet:dry* or *long:short*, are psychologically salient and have a strong associative bond between them resulting from their frequent co-occurrence (Fellbaum, 1998a). 'Indirect antonyms', then, result from similarity relations defined for the members of these direct antonym pairs. For example, *moist* and *humid* are classified as semantically similar to *wet*, and are therefore indirect antonyms of the lexeme *dry*. See Figure 2 for a schematic representation of these similarity and antonymy relations in WordNet. However, these resources do not further characterize the relations between the members of an antonymous pair. Mohammad et al. (2008) point out that WordNet does not encode the *degree* of antonymy between words; in this paper we aim to show that it is not so much the degree that should be encoded (we think that the distinction between direct and indirect antonyms already covers this for the most part), but *semantic categories* that enable distinguishing between, for example, *clear:unclear* and *appear:disappear*.

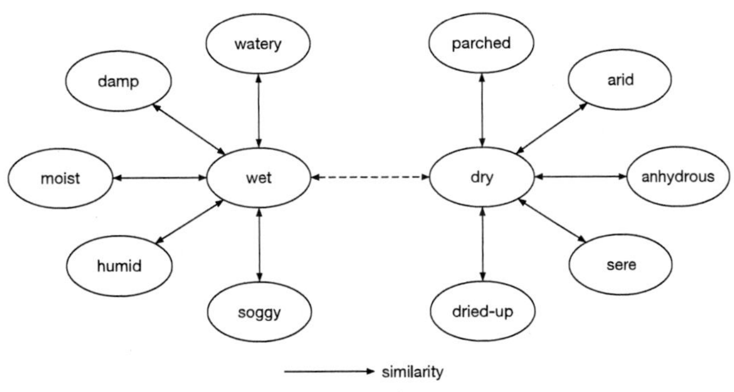


Figure 2: Similarity and antonymy relations in WordNet, from (Gross and Miller, 1990).

[1]See (Clark, 1976; Lehrer, 1985; Schriefers, 1985) and (Horn, 1989, Chapter 3) for more on the markedness of affixal negations and antonyms.

### 2.3 Semantic categories of lexical negation

As the examples in Section 2.1 illustrate, the set of affixal negations is not homogeneous. Joshi (2012) proposes grouping affixal negations into two main groups: direct and indirect. Direct negation expresses a direct opposition with its positive counterpart and "is characterized by the NOT-element in the derivative with respect to its base" (Joshi, 2012, p. 20). For example, *unhappy* can be paraphrased as *not happy*. Indirect negation, on the other hand, does not logically negate the existence of its base, yet still maintains a negative connotation (e.g. *dismount, debug*). Joshi (2012) further subcategorizes indirect negation into the types presented in Table 1. Knowledge of these subtypes is useful for making inferences about sentences containing indirect affixal negations. For example, the subtypes 'reversal of action' (e.g. in *she unlocked the door*) and 'removal' (e.g. in *dislodging a stone from the wall*) allow for inferences about previous states.

| Category | Definition | Examples |
|---|---|---|
| Reversal of direction (ROD) | Indicating movement in an opposite direction (without negating the concept of movement indicated by the base). | *diverge, decrease* |
| Reversal of action (ROA) | Indicates an action performed to reverse another previous action. | *untie, disconnect* |
| Inferiority (INF) | Indicates a lower value or quality (without negating the existence of its base). | *hypoacid, hypotension* |
| Insufficiency (INS) | Gives a precision about the level, taken as negative in some contexts. | *subnormal, underestimate* |
| Badness/wrong (WRO) | Gives a precise description of someone's behaviour in a negative way. | *miscalculate, misjudge* |
| Over-abundance (OVA) | Indicates an excessive and undesired quantity of activity. | *hyperactive, overrate* |
| Pejorative (PEJ) | Pejorative indication of excessive behaviour. | *drunkard, braggart* |
| Opposition (OPP) | Indicates an opposition in notion, action, ideology, etc. | *anti-terrorist, antimatter* |
| Removal (REM) | Indicates the removal of something. | *debug, dislodge* |

Table 1: Subtypes of indirect negation from (Joshi, 2012, p. 27). Definitions have been slightly reworded for clarity and some examples have been changed from Sanskrit or French to English for more uniformity.

Joshi's categorization system is organized in terms of the relation between the affix and the base. This can be contrasted with the taxonomy of Cruse (1986), which offers a characterization of the full domain of opposition relations between lexical items. Table 2 illustrates this, with a selection of opposition relations identified by Cruse. The overarching goal of (Cruse, 1986) is to describe the structural properties of the lexicon. Despite the differences between Joshi's and Cruse's approaches, we can also observe some similarities. For example, Cruse's category of 'reversives' strongly relates to Joshi's subtypes of 'reversal of action/direction' and 'removal'.

## 3 Building a negation dictionary

As noted by Blanco and Moldovan (2011), dealing with affixal negations seems to require a dictionary-based approach. We have shown that having a list of affixal negations may not be enough; we also need to specify the relation between the affix and the base in order to know what a word like *backless* or *miscalculate* entails. Furthermore, we have shown that affixal negations are part of a larger phenomenon that might either be called *lexical negation* (Joshi) or *lexical opposition* (Cruse). Ultimately, it seems to us that a dictionary-based approach should capture negation/opposition at this level, but creating such a dictionary goes beyond the scope of this paper. We will however take a step in this direction by testing the feasibility of creating a negation dictionary using Joshi's typology.

As a starting point for our negation dictionary, we have taken all pairs of direct antonyms from WordNet (Fellbaum, 1998b), which include both affixal negations and regular antonyms (WordNet does not make an explicit distinction between them). The full set comprises 3,557 antonym pairs and includes verbs, nouns, (satellite) adjectives and adverbs.[2]

[2]The dictionary is openly available at: `https://github.com/cltl/lexical-negation-dictionary`

| Category | Definition | Examples |
|---|---|---|
| Directions | Pairs of terms which "denoting opposite directions indicate potential paths, which, if followed by two moving lines, would result in their moving in opposite directions." | *south:north, up:down* |
| Antipodal opposites | Pairs of terms for which "one term represents an extreme in one direction along some salient axis, while the other term denotes the corresponding extreme in the other direction." | *cellar:attic, head:toe, top:bottom, source:mouth, always:never, all:none* |
| Counterparts | Pairs of terms for which one term is the counterpart of the other, "in which essential defining directions are reversed." | *ridge:groove, hill:valley* |
| Reversives | "Pairs of verbs which denote motion or change in opposite directions." | *rise:fall, ascend:descend* |
| Sub: restitutives | "Pairs one of whose members necessarily denotes the restitution of a former state." | *damage:repair, kill:resurrect* |
| Sub: independent reversives | Pairs for which "there is no necessity for the final state of either verb to be a recurrence of a former state." | *narrow:widen, fill:empty* |
| Relational opposites: converses | "Those pairs which express a relationship between two entities by specifying the direction of one relative to the other along some axis." | *above:below, before:after, teacher:pupil* |
| Sub: direct converses | "Converse pairs in which the interchangeable noun phrases occupy central valency slots." | *follow:precede* |
| Sub: indirect converses | Converse pairs "where a central and peripheral noun phrase are interchanged." | *give:receive* |

Table 2: Categories of directional oppositions from (Cruse, 1986).

### 3.1 Annotation tasks

We included the following information from WordNet about the antonym pairs in our dictionary: (1) the lemmas of both antonyms, (2) the lemma identifiers of both antonyms, (3) the definitions of both antonyms, and (4) the part of speech. Then, we performed the following three annotation steps to enrich the entries:

1. **Affixal or non-affixal:** For each antonym pair, we annotated whether the antonym pair contained an affixal negation or not. If applicable, the negative and the positive affixes were annotated as well.

2. **Direct or indirect:** For each affixal negation, we indicated whether it was a direct or an indirect negation according to the definitions provided by Joshi (2012).

3. **Subtype:** Each indirect affixal negation was classified into one of the nine subtypes defined by Joshi (2012): ROD, ROA, INF, INS, WRO, OVA, PEJ, OPP, or REM (see Table 1). In addition, we introduced a label LAC for affixal negations that indicate that some characteristic is lacking.

Table 3 shows a few simplified examples of the resulting entries in the dictionary. The tasks were performed by two annotators. A set of 500 randomly selected antonym pairs was annotated by both annotators in order to measure inter-annotator agreement.

| Positive element | Negative element | POS | Positive affix | Negative affix | Direct/indirect | Subtype |
|---|---|---|---|---|---|---|
| structured | unstructured | a | NA | un- | direct | NA |
| inshore | offshore | a | in- | off- | indirect | ROD |
| colonize | decolonize | v | NA | de- | indirect | ROA |
| revolutionary | counter-revolutionary | a | NA | counter- | indirect | OPP |
| used | misused | a | NA | mis- | indirect | WRO |
| humerously | humerlessly | r | -ous | -less | indirect | LAC |

Table 3: Simplified examples of entries of affixal negations in the dictionary (lemma identifiers and definitions are excluded for reasons of space).

### 3.2 Evaluation

Inter-annotator agreement was measured using Cohen's kappa for each of the three annotation tasks. For subtask (1), determining whether the antonym pair contained an affixal negation or not, we measured an IAA score of 0.80 (n=500). Most of the disagreements (58%) on this task were caused by mistakes of the annotators. The remaining 42% consisted of pairs where it was a bit more difficult to determine whether it should be considered an affixal negation or not. Examples are *onstage:offstage*, *intrusive:extrusive*, *concealing:revealing*. For subtask (2), indicating whether the affixal negation was direct or indirect, a rather low IAA score of 0.55 was obtained (n=268). Finally, we achieved an IAA of 0.76 (n=43) for subtask (3), the classification of indirect negations into their subtypes.

Table 4 represents the confusion matrix for the annotation of the subtypes; the 'direct' label is also included to show the disagreements between this label and each of the subtypes of indirect negation as well. What we can see from this confusion matrix is that one annotator annotated 35 antonym pairs as 'direct negation', whereas the other annotated these pairs as an indirect negation of the subtype 'opposition'. It appeared that it was not exactly clear what types of negation are covered by the 'opposition' type; although the definition provided by Joshi (2012) ("opposition in notion, action, ideology, etc.") can be understood in a very broad sense and seems similar to direct negation, the examples illustrating this subtype in (Joshi, 2012) are more specific (*anti-terrorist, antimatter*). Most of the disagreements (29/35) caused by this uncertainty regarding the definition of 'opposition' were on antonym pairs with an affixal negation starting with the prefix *non-*, such as *modern:non-modern, fictional:non-fictional, competitive:non-competitive*.

| | **LAC** | **direct** | **OPP** | **OVA/INS** | **ROA** | **ROD** | **WRO** |
|---|---|---|---|---|---|---|---|
| **INS** | 1 | 1 | 0 | 0 | 0 | 0 | 0 |
| **LAC** | **18** | 0 | 0 | 0 | 0 | 1 | 0 |
| **direct** | 0 | **179** | 35 | 0 | 3 | 1 | 0 |
| **OPP** | 0 | 0 | **1** | 0 | 0 | 0 | 0 |
| **OVA/INS** | 0 | 0 | 0 | **1** | 0 | 0 | 0 |
| **REM** | 0 | 0 | 0 | 0 | 1 | 0 | 0 |
| **ROA** | 0 | 6 | 0 | 0 | **12** | 1 | 0 |
| **ROD** | 0 | 0 | 1 | 0 | 2 | **2** | 0 |
| **WRO** | 0 | 0 | 0 | 0 | 0 | 0 | **2** |

Table 4: Confusion matrix for the annotation of subtypes

There was also some confusion between 'direct negation' and the subtype 'reversal of action', but most of them appeared to be mistakes (incorrectly annotated as 'direct'). Finally, the antonym pairs where both annotators recognized an indirect affixal negation but disagreed on the subtype were:

| **Antonym pair** | **Annotator 1** | **Annotator 2** |
|---|---|---|
| *arming:disarming* | removal | reversal of action |
| *content:discontent* | reversal of direction | reversal of action |
| *pressurise:depressurise* | reversal of direction | reversal of action |
| *conjunctive:disjunctive* | reversal of direction | opposition |
| *attachable:detachable* | reversal of action | reversal of direction |
| *merit:demerit* | lack | reversal of direction |
| *fluency:disfluency* | insufficiency | lack |

Table 5: Antonym pairs where both annotators recognized an indirect affixal negation but disagreed on the subtype.

## 4 Discussion

### 4.1 Annotating the relation between lexical items, or between affix and the base

Some words raised doubts for both annotators during the annotation process. One of these cases was the difference between the characterizations of verbal affixal negations and their inflected forms. For example, the antonym pair *fasten* ("become fixed or fastened") and *unfasten* ("become undone or untied") is a clear example of reversal of action. However, *unfastened* ("not closed or secured") seems more of a direct negation with respect to its base *fastened* ("firmly closed or secured"). The difficulty with participles like this one, which are stored as adjectives in WordNet, is that they indicate a state that can be interpreted as a result of the action expressed by its verbal base (e.g. *unfasten*) - but not necessarily (it might never have been fastened at all). Similar doubts were raised regarding antonym pairs such as *spinous* ("having spines") and *spineless* ("lacking spiny processes"). Even though the affix *-less* clearly expresses the lack of something and both annotators annotated these cases as LAC, *spineless* is just a direct negation ("not having spines") in relation to its antonym *spinous*.

Both examples are related to the question: are we annotating the relation between the affix and its base (*spine:spineless*), or the oppositional relation between the two members of an antonym pair (*spinous:spineless*)? And if we are annotating the relation between the affix and its base, what exactly should be considered the base? The simple, uninflected form (*fasten*) or the lexeme with just the negative affix stripped off (*fastened*)? These are questions that were not explicitly answered for the annotation reported in this paper, but should in fact play a central role in any future effort to build a negation dictionary.

### 4.2 Coverage

As with any lexical resource, a negation dictionary is only as good as its coverage. And since affixal negation is a productive phenomenon, we can ask ourselves: what would be a good fallback strategy to detect and reason about affixal negations? As noted by Blanco and Moldovan (2011), cited in the introduction of this paper, simple string matching algorithms will produce many false positives. One way to reduce those false positives and increase coverage might be to train a classifier (using either word-level (Mikolov et al., 2013) or character-level (Kim et al., 2016) representations) to recognize (1) whether a word has a negative component, and (2) what kind of relation exists between the affix and the base. Training such a classifier still requires us to annotate negations, however, and to think about the relations that the classifier should learn.

## 5 Conclusion

We have argued that many NLP tasks could benefit from a negation dictionary, since this would solve some of the problems that are currently encountered when detecting negations in text. One of these problems is that it is difficult to distinguish between affixal negations and words that just happen to begin with the letters of a negative prefix. However, we have shown that a simple list of affixal negations would not suffice; there is a range of different kinds of affixal negations, and which of these are relevant to include depends on the NLP task that is to be supported by the list. In addition, we have noted that, from a semantic point of view, affixal negations are not that different from negative adjectives. A dictionary that is supposed to cover the complete spectrum of lexical negation should therefore include both affixal negations and antonyms. This paper does not offer the final solution to building the perfect negation dictionary. Nevertheless, we hope that it contributes its share to the discussion by highlighting some of the main issues to be considered when building one and by proposing some elements that we think such a dictionary should minimally include: the opposing pair of lexical items with their definitions, the type of relation between them, and what affix is used (if applicable).

## 6 Acknowledgements

This work was supported by the Amsterdam Academic Alliance Data Science (AAA-DS) Program Award to the UvA and VU Universities, and by the Netherlands Organization for Scientific Research (NWO) via the Spinoza-prize awarded to Piek Vossen (SPI 30-673, 2014-2019). We also thank four anonymous reviewers for their useful feedback.

## References


Eduardo Blanco and Dan Moldovan. 2011. Some issues on detecting negation from text. In *Proceedings of the $24^{th}$ International Florida Artificial Intelligence Research Society Conference*, pages 228–233. AAAI.

Herbert H. Clark. 1976. *Semantics and Comprehension.* Mouton, The Hague.

D Alan Cruse. 1986. *Lexical semantics.* Cambridge University Press.

Christiane Fellbaum. 1998a. A semantic network of English: the mother of all WordNets. In *EuroWordNet: A multilingual database with lexical semantic networks*, pages 137–148. Springer.

Christiane Fellbaum. 1998b. *WordNet.* Wiley Online Library.

Derek Gross and Katherine J Miller. 1990. Adjectives in WordNet. *International Journal of Lexicography*, 3(4):265–277.

Laurence R. Horn. 1989. *A natural history of negation.* CSLI Publications.

Shrikant Joshi. 2012. Affixal negation – direct, indirect and their subtypes. *Syntaxe et sémantique*, (1):49–63.

Yoon Kim, Yacine Jernite, David Sontag, and Alexander Rush. 2016. Character-aware neural language models.

Adrienne Lehrer. 1985. Markedness and antonymy. *Journal of linguistics*, 21(02):397–429.

Tomas Mikolov, Kai Chen, Greg Corrado, and Jeffrey Dean. 2013. Efficient estimation of word representations in vector space. *arXiv preprint arXiv:1301.3781.*

George A Miller. 1995. WordNet: a lexical database for English. *Communications of the ACM*, 38(11):39–41.

Saif Mohammad, Bonnie Dorr, and Graeme Hirst. 2008. Computing word-pair antonymy. In *Proceedings of the Conference on Empirical Methods in Natural Language Processing*, pages 982–991. Association for Computational Linguistics.

Roser Morante and Walter Daelemans. 2012. Conan Doyleneg: Annotation of negation in Conan Doyle stories. In *Proceedings of the Eighth International Conference on Language Resources and Evaluation (LREC).*

Roser Morante, Sarah Schrauwen, and Walter Daelemans. 2011. Annotation of negation cues and their scope: Guidelines v1.0. Technical Report Series CTR-003, CLiPS, University of Antwerp, Antwerp.

Peter Mark Roget. 1911. *Roget's Thesaurus of English Words and Phrases...* TY Crowell Company.

Heribert Johannes Schriefers. 1985. On semantic markedness in language production and verification.

Michael Wiegand, Alexandra Balahur, Benjamin Roth, Dietrich Klakow, and Andrés Montoyo. 2010. A survey on the role of negation in sentiment analysis. In *Proceedings of the Workshop on Negation and Speculation in Natural Language Processing*, pages 60–68. Association for Computational Linguistics.

# Author Index

**Association for Computational Linguistics**
209 N. Eighth Street
Stroudsburg, Pennsylvania 18360

ISBN 978-1-5108-3330-2

CURRAN ASSOCIATES INC.
proceedings.com